Forgetting Former Things
The Power of Letting Go

Brenda Murphy

(BSB) – The Holy Bible, Berean Study Bible, BSB; Copyright ©2016 by Bible Hub; Used by permission. All Rights Reserved Worldwide.

(ESV) – Scripture quotations are from The ESV® Bible (The Holy Bible, English Standard Version®), copyright © 2001 by Crossway, a publishing ministry of Good News Publishers. Used by permission. All rights reserved.

(KJV) – The Holy Bible, King James Version. Cambridge Edition: 1769; King James Bible Online, 2018. www.kingjamesbibleonline.org.

(MSG) – Scripture quotations marked MSG are taken from THE MESSAGE, copyright © 1993, 1994, 1995, 1996, 2000, 2001, 2002 by Eugene H. Peterson. Used by permission of NavPress. All rights reserved. Represented by Tyndale House Publishers, Inc.

(NASB) – Scripture quotations taken from the New American Standard Bible® (NASB), Copyright © 1960, 1962, 1963, 1968, 1971, 1972, 1973, 1975, 1977, 1995 by The Lockman Foundation Used by permission. www.Lockman.org

(NIV) – Scripture quotations marked (NIV) are taken from the Holy Bible, New International Version®, NIV®. Copyright © 1973, 1978, 1984, 2011 by Biblica, Inc.™ Used by permission of Zondervan. All rights reserved worldwide. www.zondervan.com The "NIV" and "New International Version" are trademarks registered in the United States Patent and Trademark Office by Biblica, Inc.™

(NKJV) – Scripture taken from the New King James Version®. Copyright © 1982 by Thomas Nelson. Used by permission. All rights reserved.

(NLT) – Scripture quotations marked (NLT) are taken from the Holy Bible, New Living Translation, copyright ©1996, 2004, 2015 by Tyndale House Foundation. Used by permission of Tyndale House Publishers, Inc., Carol Stream, Illinois 60188. All rights reserved.

Copyright © 2018 Brenda Murphy

Publisher: bylisabell
Radical Women
(DBA)
PO Box 782
Granbury, TX
76048
www.bylisabell.com

The opinions, beliefs and viewpoints expressed by the author of this book may not necessarily reflect the opinions, beliefs and viewpoints of Radical Women.

All rights reserved.

ISBN:10: 0-9983308-7-6
ISBN-13: 978-0-9983308-7-7

Dedication

Over two years ago, I was sitting in a church service waiting in anticipation for another incredible Word from the Lord when suddenly, at least to me, this woman was introduced as the speaker for the hour. I had never heard her preach before. I remember that particular day when she opened her mouth, the power of God drew me in with intention and I knew in that particular moment my personal life was being called into divine order, so I listened very carefully.

Every other time she preached the Word of God in my hearing, I was intrigued, captivated and eager to hear more. I realized in each of those moments, this wasn't just a random word being spoken but rather it was alive, purposeful and deliberate, and it left me personally hungry for the next spiritual meal.

From that time forward, each time I was privileged to hear the Word of the Lord being birthed through this vessel of God into my life, I knew I was being moved to change very rapidly and it caused me to become inspired to pursue God like my life depended upon it, because spiritually speaking—I understood it does.

Today, I would like to publically acknowledge and thank this incredible, dynamic God filled woman who speaks with holy boldness and carries over her life a tremendous anointing.

Thank you **Dr. Veronica Cochran** *for your encouragement and enlightenment. Your spoken seeds over my life ignited such a flame of urgency, discipline and greater cause of responsibility in my life that will never go out, but rather causes me to move forward in a spirit of wisdom, focus and victory. At the end of the day, I know that He knows my name.*

Sincerely,
Brenda Murphy

Table of Contents

Acknowledgments i

The Power of Forgiveness ii

Introduction viii

Section I: The Power of Forgiveness xv

    Chapter 1 – The Definition of Anguish 2

    Chapter 2 – Is Letting Go Really Possible? 4

    Chapter 3 – Remembering It like It Was Yesterday 12

    Chapter 4 – How Do You Let Go of The Past? 30

Section II: Trusting God No Matter What 54

    Chapter 5 – Can Things Get Any Worse? 55

    Chapter 6 – Where Was God in All of My Suffering and Pain? 64

    Chapter 7 – Now, What Do I Do? 88

    Chapter 8 – Is Forgiveness Necessary? 91

Section III: The Choice to Move Forward 98

    Chapter 9 – What Was the Purpose of the Pain? 99

    Chapter 10 – Struggling With Suffering Is Real 106

    Chapter 11 – The God Who Suffered On My Behalf 118

    Chapter 12 – Looking Ahead Through a Different Perspective
.... 129

Section IV: Keeping Your Eyes on the Important Prize 135

    Chapter 13 – Don't Cast Away Your Confidence in God 136

    Chapter 14 – Trust God with Your Past as You Move Forward Into Your Promising Future 147

    Chapter 15 – Decide There Will Be No More Wasted Energy . 154

Chapter 16 – It's Working for Your Good 161

Section V: Casting All of Our Cares Upon God 170

Chapter 17 – The Sweet Side of Victory! 171

Chapter 18 – No More Delays 176

Chapter 19 – Empowering Quotes for the Soul 187

Chapter 20 – Overview 189

Section VI: The Final Decision Is Up To You 212

Chapter 21 – Final Words; Think on These Things 213

Chapter 22 - Becoming Kingdom Minded For Kingdom Purpose 224

Chapter 23 - Personal Take-a-Ways 229

References 259

About the Author 261

"But I say unto you, Love your enemies, bless them that curse you, do good to them that hate you, and pray for them which despitefully use you, and persecute you."
Matthew 5:44 (KJV)

Acknowledgments

I would like to personally thank all of the countless beautiful and courageous people in my life whom I greatly love, cherish, admire and am so thankful for. You have lovingly supported, guided and prayed for me and gently nudged and reinforced positive change into my life that will continue to serve as a spiritual springboard for me to continue to grow, expand and blossom into the will and purpose of God. Your strong sense of encouragement, motivation and genuine care and concern for me will continue to serve as the catalyst to which I will continue to sprint forward in becoming the person God has designed for my life

Love Always,
Brenda

The Power of Forgiveness

Not that I have already obtained all this, or have already been perfected, but I press on to take hold of that for which Christ Jesus took hold of me. Brothers, I do not consider myself yet to have laid hold of it. But one thing I do: Forgetting what is behind and straining toward what is ahead, I press on toward the goal to win the prize of God's heavenly calling in Christ Jesus.

Philippians 3:12-14 *(NLT)*

Wow! There it was right there in front of me. Starring me in the face all this time—the freedom I desired. The liberty I craved for real peace I so desperately needed. I didn't fully understand how to lay hold of it permanently and how to allow myself to be aligned with the sheer peace of God for my personal journey.

Looking back today, I couldn't believe how many hours, weeks, months and even years I allowed my life to be rearranged, tossed to and fro, turned upside down at certain pinnacles—all to appease the actions, circumstances and sometimes the situations of others.

Shamefully, at times, I allowed someone else's views or their opinions of me to override what I knew about myself even if I wasn't 100% confident in that particular moment about my gift or abilities to complete the job. Not realizing it, my fears allowed doubt to take over way before I sometimes gave my all at moving forward.

Still, given what I know now, I should never have allowed myself to drink from that off-centered, indecisive cup the enemy so carefully offered up to me. However, in that moment, I didn't know any better. I unknowingly, and sometimes urgently feeling the need to defend myself; responded to the enemy's deliberate tactics, when truly I should have simply pulled back and gave it much thought before advancing into the enemies snare head on.

Many times, I walked around, unfortunately for several months, beating myself up, hanging on to unnerving, hurtful and slanderous accusations and comments. These did not pertain to nor apply to the person nor the character of the person God created me to be. Yet, focusing too much on hurtful words, I allowed their comments to wound me both inside and out.

Even right now, I constantly forgive myself for the long, bitter and unnecessary winters I endured because I did not always use my godly wisdom to fight back or to stand in His truth over my life. Even then, I allowed someone else's opinion of me to temporarily matter most, at times, to my costly detriment

In hindsight, I shouldn't have even allowed the snares from the enemy's bad breath to remotely penetrate my emotions, let alone my heart, and distort the wonderful view God has for my life.

I should have recognized that the picture the enemy showed to the world and me came from an amateur artist's camera at best, and that the photos would be revealed as being distorted and out of focus. The enemy knows he will never ever be able to capture the joy, empowerment and gifting God put inside of me—for my good and his defeat.

Now I know I should have just kept moving forward even if the vision wasn't as clear as it is now. Still, I didn't recognize the answer, and I didn't know the true get out of jail card I only needed stared me right in the face the whole time.

Would you like to know the real answer for me today? In a nutshell, it was and is the Power of Forgiveness. Over the years, I worked with some of the most intriguing, talented and, perhaps in their own right, powerful individuals as well as some amazing CEOs.

I had the pleasure of watching millionaires grow and unfortunately, on some personal level, I also witnessed some of them fall. But I never really understood how that happened. They were very smart, wealthy, well-versed, well known and to some degree, very well loved or at least liked individuals. But still, I didn't know until…

Yes, you guess it; there it is again, the Power of Forgiveness. You may ask, "What does the power of forgiveness have to do with anything?" My friend, you may be amazed as to how you and I can't afford to truly move forward freely without it.

Oh sure, it might be easy to move out of someone's house and move to a different location and call it a home. However, what you didn't factor in was one of the most prized possessions you left behind—your broken heart. The upheaval of your emotions and inability to have confidence in who you are as a person that you left behind will continually haunt you, until you make true amends.

Sure, you can hop in the car and speed off, determining never to look back at your old life again, or determining to get on with the next chapter of your life, vowing not to allow anyone else in this world to hurt you ever again.

However, you forgot one small oversight. When you jumped in the car, those mean-spirited comments you left behind, the hurtful words you allowed to spew out of your mouth before you got in the car, or the shame and degradation you felt on your part of the unforgiveness still lingers until this day. They all remain with you.

Perhaps you may have forgotten about the things you uttered in that moment when it didn't matter to you what you said, who may have heard you when you spoke the words, or who saw or knew you.

You didn't care whether the whole world knew, because you were done. You limped off in the night, licking tender wounds and bandaging them from sight. Finished—or so you thought—with the entire situation.

When you got in the car, you didn't factor in one important truth. Unfortunately, on the other side of the car, in the passenger seat, unforgiveness waited to go with you, and maybe unbeknownst to you, together you both drove into the next chapter of your life, bound hand and hand.

Perhaps you never realized forgiveness wasn't reviewed as an option. In order for you to be completely set free and rid of the old shackles and bondages that literally drain all of the life, joy, substances and peace from your human spirit, you can't refuse to forgive.

Understanding that when one chooses to forgive and rid themselves of all the old clutter of bitterness, hatred, shame and hurt caused by others, or perhaps self-inflicting wounds, it doesn't matter. They all fall under the same category of the power of forgiveness by which a victim undergoes a change in feelings and attitude regarding an offense.

> "Now, I understand that peace doesn't come in a prepackaged gift that only needs to be unwrapped once; instead, peace is something that I will always have to contend for all the remainder of my days in Jesus' Name!"
>
> Brenda Murphy

Letting go of negative emotions and baggage through forgiveness is the letting go of grudges and bitterness that have become so detrimentally rooted inside that it can stunt the growth of any future life-giving opportunities to move ahead and live your best life ever.

The other important thing I learned about the power of forgiveness is that it provides you with the last laugh. When you freely forgive yourself and others, you are agreeing with God that what he has in store for you is far more worthy, powerful and better than holding on to meaningless and unproductive energy and time wasted you could have better spent living in the pursuit, purpose and plan to which God called you.

When we choose the power of forgiveness, we generously deliver the enemy a blow to the ego he never, ever expected to see coming. We take back the proverbial keys to rid ourselves of the man-made shackles or bondages that held us back from living far too long. In fact, he looks for ways in which to keep us bound, shackled and locked up in a sea of lies and trepidation we may never recognized as ill will toward us.

However, once we discover for ourselves the real liberty and freedom that comes through the power of forgiveness, we will undoubtedly discover what really living and enjoyment is all about! It's the true freedom only our God can bring about in our lives.

> *"Always forgive your enemies; nothing annoys them so much."*
>
> Oscar Wilde

Introduction

In *A Glimpse of Jesus,* Brennan Manning quotes philosopher Blaise Pascal. "God made man in His own image, and man returned the compliment."[1] If we are conservative, we tend to think of God as being conservative. If we are mad at the world, we may feel that God is mad at the world, too.

Interestingly enough, what I now know for sure is that God's perfect timing in my life cannot be disputed, rewritten, challenged, changed or denied. What He speaks is so and that's the end of that story and chapter.

I remember it like it was only yesterday. At a specific era in my young adult life, I came to a conclusion that I was not totally happy. Even though according to the scriptures, I was 100% set free by the blood of Jesus Christ, it was noticeable at times I was not always walking nor resting in that incredible peace given to me.

I could not understand how at times I was happy as a lark. Then at other times, in the presence of negative people or those not necessarily pleasant to be around, I made it a point to avoid them like the plague. I always felt uneasy being around their negative comments and feedback.

Though at times, no matter how hard I desired peace and joy, life matters or reasoning seemingly out of my control, timing, reach or fate somehow always abruptly

---

[1] (Manning, 2004)

interrupted my peace. At least at the time, that was what I believed.

There were mornings I got out of bed being determined this was the day I was going to live totally victorious. I was for sure going to make an impact, a statement, and a difference. At the very least, I would prove to others my life had changed, and I was totally in love with Jesus. More importantly, He loved me more than I could ever love Him.

One big problem. As long as I surrounded myself with like-minded people or my circumstances lined up with my thinking and everything went my way, life was grand. However, I didn't factor in one important ingredient that always showed, ready or not, here it comes, yes, you guessed it, life happened. And I found myself swindled again back into some of the same old patterns of thoughts, reactions and sometimes even the same mindsets.

I was saved, and I knew it. A significant change truly took place in my life—that I was well aware of. Not only did I notice it right away, I felt it on the inside in real time. Even though a real difference happened in my spiritual life and I was excited. I welcomed the change immediately, but no one ever taught me that life keeps coming at you each and every day, saved or not.

I didn't necessarily know exactly how to let go of my entire past. All of my underlying issues, concerns, fears that consumed me and deliberately turn everything over to God for the long haul. I mean within myself, I made every attempt to put what I thought was my best foot forward. Still life chased me down daily, and sometimes I allowed my feelings to get the best of me. Then my emotions wasted no time in reminding me who I used to be just a few short years, months, weeks—heck, even days before.

Even though I wasn't necessarily a newborn babe in Christ, I still had a lot to learn. I continue to grow until this day and strive for letting things go. I'm not fully able to digest everything that comes at me in one setting, even being born again and reading my bible often. One thing I knew for sure was I wanted to be and feel free totally with no subliminal strings attached. I like the spiritual taste of being free in Christ and receiving all He has for me.

I didn't know at the time that God gave me total peace and tranquility through His son Jesus on the cross at Calvary. A peace never to be exchanged or rented out to the enemy. An enemy who wants to keep me consumed in a rhythm of unresolved issues with stems growing over a period of time in my life from childhood, adolescent years and even at times, spilling over into adulthood.

I couldn't make the spiritual connection after becoming a daughter of the Most High and still being plagued at times with raw emotions of pain, hurt, sorrow, and defeat when I thought about all I came through over the years. After I became a Christian, someone said being born again would bring a new sense of being free—that I would not have to worry about being hurt or wounded because God took care of all of that.

So imagine when those emotions came in droves. After a while, I was confused and my feelings reflected so. At times, I questioned why this was happening to me. Until one day, thank God for Jesus, I heard the Holy Spirit speak to me, "Daughter, he that the Son sets free, is free indeed." (John 8:36)

I remember crying and saying, "Lord, I desperately want that kind of peace in my life."

Hearing those words, I earnestly asked, "Father God, please show me how to receive that for myself. I desire your ultimate peace." Thus, the challenge to walk in that freedom continuously has been ongoing for me from that time forward, even to this day.

Freedom, according to Dictionary.com, states that it is the power or right to act, speak, or think as one wants without hindrance or restraint. And looking at "freedom" through the lenses of the worlds ideas of freedom from this statement makes it a fact. Look around you today at the world's repercussions and aftermath, horror stories of our abilities to speak, act, and perform in any manner we choose with very minimum backlash or accountability.

However, as we look through the lens of our Almighty God, true freedom is viewed differently and, more importantly, more profoundly. Through God's truth, which overrides and trumps mankind's lack of wisdom and understanding of freedom, we see a greater knowledge and stronger foundation in which to base our entire lives on. For instance, let's take a look at John 8:32, the scripture that reads, *"And ye shall know the truth, and the truth shall make you free." (KJV)*

Essentially, freedom or freedom that is vital to our very being does not come to us just by repeating or saying the words "I am free" over and over again." True freedom does not happen just because we choose to march and wear certain attire and chant the words of "Free indeed, free indeed, thank God Almighty we are free in deed" – Dr. Martin Luther King.

True freedom ensues in the person who understands and believes their sin is acquitted, pardoned, forgiven and dealt with once and for all at the foot of the cross by way of Jesus Christ's willingness to die for us.

Each of us, if we are born again, can receive and accept the reality of Christ dying on the cross and footing the entire bill for all of our sins and acknowledging Him as our Lord and Savior. And then, we can choose to live a very free, fruitful and productive life while living here on earth.

However, understand we will *make many mistakes.* But when we *repent and turn away from that with God's help*, and ask Him for strength and wisdom to do better as we continue living out loud for Him. And after we die, we will still reflect that Jesus Christ has paid it all!

Although for a lot of Christians today, they still struggle with the notion that all of their sins have been paid for by Jesus Christ and they struggle with what they can do to help repay the remainder of the balance due for their sins. They may think, surely I have to do something, right? No one just does something this great for me, and I don't owe him anything?

Well, not exactly. While there are no balances due for the payment that our Lord and Savior have already paid on the Cross, we are still responsible for how we render services to each other. We are charged to love one another as Christ loves us. *"A new command I give you: Love one another. As I have loved you, so you must love one another."* John 13:34 (NIV)

Likewise, Ephesians 3:42 charges us to *"Be kind and compassionate to one another, forgiving each other, just as in Christ, God forgave you."* (NIV) These commands are not just great ideas. They are expected of us as born-again believers—even if it hurts our flesh or when we are too stubborn to admit we are wrong and continuously hang on things that hurt us five or more years ago.

It is more than just an assumption or a great idea. Jesus paid it all for all sinners. To the believer and the potential sinners alike, we need to embrace fully the fact that death is vanquished. The prince of this world is cast out.

Today, let's choose to believe and receive the good news that as sons and daughters of the Most High God, we are "free indeed," whatever the world, or the Hebrew Christians, or the philosophers might think or say.

Sin shall not have dominion over you: for ye are not under the law, but under grace. What then? Shall we sin, because we are not under the law, but under grace? God forbid. Romans.6:14-15 KJV —My brethren, ye… are become dead to the law by the body of Christ; that ye should be married to another, even to him who is raised from the dead, that we should bring forth fruit unto God.—Being not without law to God, but under the law to Christ.--The sting of death is sin; and the strength of sin is the law.

Anonymous—Daily Light on the Daily Path

Section I:
The Power
of Forgiveness

Chapter 1 – The Definition of Anguish

The definition of anguish according to the King James Bible Page (taken from the public domain version of *Webster's American Dictionary of the English Language, 1828*) is an "extreme pain, either of body or mind. Anguish is a bodily pain that may differ from agony, which is such distress of the whole body as to cause contortion, whereas anguish may be a local pain as of an ulcer, or some other disease.

"But anguish and agony are nearly synonymous. As pain of the mind, it signifies any keen distress from sorrow, remorse, despair and kindred passions."[2]

Likewise, Vocabulary.com describes anguish as a word "we get from a Latin term called, angustus, which literally meant "narrow" but developed the figurative sense of "distressed" — think of being choked off or forced into a small space.

"In modern times *anguish* has been in English with

---

[2] (Webster, n.d.)

the parallel and related meanings of "physical torment" and "emotional suffering." Both kinds might be experienced at the hands of a dentist who likes to make his patients squirm in agony."[3]

Technical definitions are great. But I have a different perspective.

> "I personally describe anguish as being fear wrapped into doubt designed to stop or snuff out the flow of God's purpose in our lives at any cost and by any method or means necessary."
>
> Brenda Murphy

---

[3] (Thinkmap, Inc, n.d.)

Chapter 2 – Is Letting Go Really Possible?

Do not call to mind the former things, Or ponder things of the past. Behold, I will do something new, now it will spring forth; will you not be aware of it? I will even make a roadway in the wilderness, Rivers in the desert.

Isaiah 43:18-19 (NASB)

I am a firm believer that absolutely nothing good, promising, profitable or beneficial comes from holding on to our pasts—torturing ourselves about the mental pains and anguish as well as the pertinent details about who hurt us, who left us, who overlooked us, who said and did what to us.

Failing to see or understand that each time we allow our minds to pay homage to those low places in our minds and permeate our hearts, we potentially halt the progress of the wound ever standing a chance of healing.

Therefore, the cycle of all the pain, betrayal and backlash of it all starts over again with a new starting date of the hurt more vividly remembered. Then the chances of its damaging affects become deeper than previously noted. Dwelling on the wound opens the door to drudgery, which causes the proverbial wounds of our past pains to never close permanently. And it keeps us bound to that individual, circumstance or mental situation longer than necessary, which often shackles us and renders us as a hostage in our own minds.

If unresolved issues are not dealt with, they often keep resurfacing over and over in our lives. Finally, when it appears all of our energy and strength has been exasperated to no end, the weight of it all can drag us off to that dark, unhealthy place in us that we prayed so hard to escape in the first place.

To me, pain is a place where several emotions range. In some ways, pain can be a benefit to our wellbeing. If we allow the process of walking through pain to teach us valuable and necessary life lessons, we can grow from it. Quite frankly, pain can also bring about the worst outcome we could ever imagine and leave us wondering, "Where did that response or reaction from within me come from?"

Pain has a way of excavating old wounds from our path that we may have thought were dead, well-hidden and deeply buried both out of sight and out of mind. If not dead, totally forgotten by all. If the issues of our past weren't dead and buried already, we thought perhaps they were at least locked away in a comatose state.

No matter how much we try to fake it until we make it, pain has a way of kicking back the dirt from its old dusty casket, clearing the cobwebs and climbing out of the grave. Ridding itself away from its self-made casket of our souls, pain wreaks havoc in our current lives, causing old emotions to resurface. With a new and refreshed vengeance, it has an insatiable appetite designed to hurt anyone who enters its path.

Until pain is completely rendered helpless, it can leave a devastating path so treacherous and unnerving that it can disturb even the most well-mannered, even tempered, well put together person in the world without the least bit of notice.

Take the most recent shootings around the world where more than enough evidence indicated that some white police officers deliberately took the lives of unarmed young and old black men and women. No other reason seemed evident than the victims' skin color. They may have felt they had the power to do so due to their badges and possibly face no adverse consequences from those in authority over them. The shootings happened.

Never once stopping to think or care about the pain they inflicted on countless of people who watched, witnessed, and heard about their seeming intentional hatred strewed out around the world. Not only the undeserved pain but also additionally a national disgrace of disgust and anguish. The actions of some bad men caused a national outrage that at times, could not be contained.

The pain of all the hatred and deliberate attacks, in

my opinion alone, sent a blatant message to the world that tried to indicate a certain race and imagery was in control of the universe. Thankfully and prayerfully, not all of every race applauded the enemy's ill-willed plan. Many showed their support, love and dedication to the real cause—to show love in spite of hatred.

Still, in its aftermath, the devastation left behind tremendous pain and sorrow to insurmountable families. Relationships, as well as children, may take years or decades to be reconciled or healed from its aftermath. Some may never heal. Unfortunately, for some families, they were left without any respectable closure or goodbyes to their love ones.

To me, that's pain one-on-one. To hear others saying we should stop the violence and remain calm took a lot of prayer and effort on my part. My flesh was on edge, at least in my thoughts.

I thought, perhaps they don't have a television or a radio. Maybe they are not aware of all the social media that exists throughout our world today. How could they not see details upon details of footage being shown through the day and well into the nights? And even suggest that as other races, we should simply remain calm, really? You think so?

Quite frankly, I was grieved to see people of color having to hold up signs and volunteering their time in walking the street before the world chanting "Black Lives Matter." With tears streaming down my face, sadness in my heart, all I could say at one point was, "Really?" Are we reverting back to the days of Martin Luther King when he gave the "I Have a Dream" speech?

Honestly, here we are in 2016 and individuals who put on a badge of authority, arm themselves with weaponry and take oaths to protect and swear to be governed by the law. Yet they easily, effortlessly and intentionally break their own laws and stand not even the chance of a little punishment no matter how much video, snapshots, Facebook or national news headlines appear.

Regardless of how the loss happens, I cannot even begin to imagine the pain and anguish of those mothers and fathers who have to live with various losses of their children or in some cases, their spouses and other love ones. Imagine, one act of hate put another family at a greater risk by taking away that home's provider, covering, protector and that tremendous gap they once filled at the family table.

Pain can indeed render us hopeless and disheartened, especially in that moment of time when the news is fresh and newly revealed. Often when news of a death or the loss of a job, breakup of a marriage or a friend, family member or even a co-worker betrayal, it can really steal our joy and rob us of peace in God if allowed.

The pain and the residue from it all can leave behind the loneliness that often embraces us like a cold, damp blanket left out in the open elements overnight. Pain can cause us to retreat and retract those things that we were once confident in just moments earlier. When caught off guard, pain, has a way of causing us to second guess the very state of our being.

While it is definitely not easy to just forget about those specific moments, it is necessary if we are going to move forward in being determined to lead a much healthier, wholesome and healed lifestyle. One of the most successful ways I found in moving forward is simply making a decision—a conscious choice. Reading the Word of God daily assists me in reaching my goal.

It is my hope that through reading this book, you begin to find your own personal path. In making that necessary and gratifying decision for yourself, personally ask God for the strength, determination and decision to move forward in beginning again. With a fresh start, I pray you take this journey with me and countless others, healing both inside and out.

In response to the original question asked at the beginning of this chapter, "Is it really possible to let it go?" Had this very question been asked of me years ago, I am sure my response would have been something totally different than what it is today. It would have probably went something like this, "Yes, but it would be extremely difficult to do so."

My reasoning perhaps for responding in such a manner would be because at the time, my perspective was totally different. My response would be coming directly from my flesh more so than my heart because of the freshness of it all. I would have been looking for closure in all the wrong places.

I now understand that it doesn't matter what someone

did, said or how he or she treated me. Whether it was in a disrespectful, unpleasant and unprofessional manner, it is still up to me to **decide** to forgive them in my heart and not allow what they did to me to fester and become a spiritual eyesore in my body.

I would be absolutely correct in saying "Yes, but it would be extremely difficult to do so," because in a roundabout way, I choose to hold on to the hurt, anger and perhaps disappointment a little longer than I should or longer than necessary. Still, that's a deliberate decision I choose to make.

I heard a statement a while back by Bishop T. D. Jakes that said, *"You cannot become offended by something someone said to you or about you unless you choose to carry that offense around with you."*

In other words, I am in control over whether or not I allow others' words—whether right or wrong—control and have dominion over me. While I know words can deliberately bless me or harm me as well as build me up, even if the motive of the wording is conceived in love. I can allow words of hatred and destruction to cause me to retaliate and respond back in the same like manner accomplishing absolutely nothing.

The good news, is if the words are coming from a place of destruction and deceit, I need to be what I call armored up. In making sure I am wearing my protective gear. The apostle Paul describes the whole Armor of God.

Finally, my brethren, be strong in the Lord and in the power of His might. Put on the whole armor of God that you may be able to stand against the wiles of the devil, for we do not wrestle against flesh and blood, but against principalities, against powers, against the rulers of the darkness of this age, against spiritual hosts of wickedness in the heavenly places. Therefore, take up the whole armor of God that you may be able to withstand in the evil day, and having done all, to stand.

Stand therefore, having girded your waist with truth, having put on the breastplate of righteousness, and having shod your feet with the preparation of the gospel of peace; above all, taking the shield of faith with which you will be able to quench all the fiery darts of the wicked one.

And take the helmet of salvation, and the sword of the Spirit, which is the word of God; praying always with all prayer and supplication in the Spirit, being watchful to this end with all perseverance and supplication for all the saints— and for me, that utterance may be given to me, that I may open my mouth boldly to make known the mystery of the gospel, for which I am an ambassador in chains; that in it I may speak boldly, as I ought to speak.

Ephesians 6:10-20 (NKJV)

Chapter 3 – Remembering It like It Was Yesterday

Brethren, I count not myself to have apprehended: but this one thing I do, forgetting those things which are behind, and reaching forth unto those things which are before, I press toward the mark for the prize of the high calling of God in Christ Jesus.

Philippians 3:13-14 (KJV)

When I first came across this specific scripture in the Bible, I literally chose to skip over the entire chapter because there was nothing in me that was ready to accept its truth at the time. I wasn't ready to remotely let any of my accuser's off the hook, let alone give them a free pass, or ignore the fact that they robbed me of my peace, stole my joy, and at that moment they were gaining serious ground on sabotaging my sanity.

Some days just the mention of their names, even when they were nowhere around, made my stomach turn in anguish, because I *remembered* every minute detail of what they said. I envisioned what they looked like when they were saying the words. I *remembered* how they smelled when they approached me—the smell of malice and trepidation. I remembered their menacing body language through the demonic pleasure they took in speaking to me in such a demeaning undertone as though they were superior to me and over me. At other times, they attempted to demote me as if they had the authority to do so.

There were times when I *remembered* little attempts that didn't work out to their advantage. They felt the need to filter their deceit through other available methods or unsuspecting victims, to participate in what looked to be my downfall. Through their subtle remarks made often in public, they belittled or diminished me, causing me to feel small or invaluable in their eyes. Thank God their eyes weren't that big, if you understand what I mean.

For some of those individuals, I could tell that they really labored intensely over what they were going to say; how they would say it, and of course timing of their unflattering words. It was all about the timing of it all. Perhaps they may have thought I was too infantile to understand that the joke or the insult was meant for my harm rather than my good. Nevertheless, and to no avail, it didn't stop that person from taking advantage of every moment or opportunity to do so.

As the negative treatment from some grew, I found myself withdrawing from the group because I was extremely shy by nature anyway, and I did not enjoy confrontation of any kind. In fact, I was the polar opposite. I did everything within my power to stay away from any conflict and discord. Nevertheless, the more I shied away, the more intensified the discord continued.

While in my early childhood and even into young adulthood, I rarely looked anyone in the face when talking with him or her, and what made it even worse, I was an exceptionally soft speaker. I thought that I spoke in an average volume range in what I called normal conversations. Little did I know, others found having a conversation with me extremely frustrating because some said they barely understood a word that I said.

I was however intelligent, and I loved to approach a subject matter from every angle. I was, and still am to this day, a detailed oriented kind of person. I love truth and what it stands for.

I had to learn that not everyone is about the truth. Why? Well, because most lies are just easier to accept and repeat and therefore easily transferrable. Plus, the one common benefit to lies and liars is that they always make headlines faster than the Road Runner could say *"Beep-Beep!"*

I prided myself on treating others "right" as my mother would often say to me. *"Baby, whatever you do in life; don't forget to treat others right and right will always follow you."* While her words were true, it doesn't make the process or the ability to do so easy to carry out. In fact, it seemed at times, the more I tried to "treat people *right*" the more I endured others taking advantage of me.

I love to dream big dreams and always imagined

myself being successful in some capacity in the world. I never liked to waste my energy or time on things that were not vital, or things that didn't make a tremendous difference or add value to others or me.

In fact, one of my greatest joys in the world is making a difference in the lives of others. I get a jolt of excitement when others' days are made, and they are surprised their prayers and dreams were answered. It is so rewarding and refreshing to see.

So in that vein, I never allowed myself to become familiar with the word quitting because that was never my goal or my habit. Neither was it ever an option for me personally. I believe I can do all things through Christ Jesus who strengthens me.

The words quit and defeat are words—just a part of my vocabulary or terminology. To simply grab hold and accept them? No. At least not until I exhausted all options provided to me. I never made it a point to embrace the word quitting nor hold it as a term of endearment.

I knew that if I didn't vote for me in life, whom else could I really depend upon to do so? I challenged myself to keep pressing passed the obstacles and the temporary setbacks through the doubts and fears. I was, and still am today, determined, persistent and prone to trust in God no matter what.

If I didn't have anything else going for me, I believed that through reading and absorbing the Word of God, brighter days ahead remained—as long as I continued to steady the course and walk in the vision until I could readily lay my hands on God's provision for life through my faith.

I also believed trusting and depending upon God and His word for my life would inevitably be well. I was, and am still, very much determined to finish strong. I know with God at the helm of my life, I will continue to thrive and develop under the Mighty hand of God all of the days of my appointed time here in the earth. I choose to believe I will see tremendous progress in my life and the life of my family.

Admittedly, though at times, it was extremely difficult lugging all of life's dead weight of what others thought of me around. Glimpsing back through time, I cannot believe I wasted unnecessary time and excessive energy even caring about what others said about me, or for that matter even thought about me.

What I hadn't realize at that point in my life was that I could have let it all go. All of the negativity, hurt, pain and disappointments. My times were never in the hands of others. But I didn't have a solid understanding of that wisdom, and I allowed the enemy to move into my heart with his lies of being "hurt and offended" by it all. Then I simply camped out for a while.

The other sad fact I didn't take into consideration was that in those times when you have been wounded and hurt by others, it isn't wise to remain around the same people who hurt or wounded you—especially when you are trying to make things right and they have not changed. You have to move out and sometimes away from the wreckage if for nothing else than your peace and sanctity.

Looking back years later, I wish I recognized the signs and started the process of healing much earlier. And the process of letting it go and releasing all that negativity to God, trusting Him with the blueprint for the very fiber of my life. I wish I learned sooner the outcome of His will for my purpose instead of indulging in the false advertising of the enemy time and time again.

I didn't know or fully grasp the fact that I could have erased the negative tape and negative thoughts replaying itself over and over again in my head through the deliverance of the blood of Jesus. Knowing what I know now, I could have canceled the taping of those old reruns from the enemies' camp anytime I wanted to with the right weapons of the Word of God.

> *For though we live in the flesh, we do not wage war according to the flesh; The weapons of our warfare are not the weapons of the world. Instead, they have divine power to demolish strongholds. We tear down arguments, and every presumption set up against the knowledge of God; and we take captive every thought to make it obedient to Christ.*
>
> 2 Corinthians 10:3-5 (BSB)

Sure, I followed along in the Word of God when I heard the Pastors talk about *"laying it all at the alter"* or *"giving it all to Jesus."* Don't laugh when I say this, but I really thought I was doing just that—until I noticed, usually driving on the way home from church, work or the supermarket, my anger looked like an emotional roller-coaster. At times going from highs to mid-lows, but sometimes, they even came out just when I thought I had dealt with a certain situation and mentally moved passed the previous disappointments of it all. Now, I realize all I had done was suppressed my emotions and tried to deal with them on some form of human emotional level on my own.

There were times, it was a real struggle for me to get over some of the harsh words and actions of what other people said and thought of me. I cannot speak for others on this subject matter. However, I find it difficult at best when someone lies on you to others and in spite of knowing your true character, they believe what the individual said.

Sometimes it is even more challenging to move forward when you are face-to-face with those individuals at least several times during any given day or week—especially when you are trying everything you can to walk in peace and take the high road so as not to stoop to their level.

Over time, I began to really dig deeper into the Word of God and cried out to him alone for total release and total liberty in His Holy Name. I didn't just merely want to be "fixed" or "mended," I wanted complete and total healing. I wanted to be free and rid of everything and everyone I had allowed to keep me bound.

I came to the conclusion over time, that if I was going to make it in this society, I'd better toughen up and start speaking up for myself as it relates to God's truth about me and not the word of the enemy trying to reign over me riddling my life with his false reports and judgments.

In time, I learned how to counteract the attacks of the enemy through the Living Word of God and not to be moved by what I saw, heard or felt. Daily, I began to understand the power of my thoughts as well as my responses. Through the Word of God, I learned I owed the devil no explanation about his ill-will comments or deeds.

As I consistently made the Word of God a priority in my life, I found myself over the years speaking God's truth over my life instead of trying to validate or refute the enemy's lies just because of his deliberate attacks against me or those I loved.

For example, whenever the enemy said something negative, I immediately said out loud what the Word of God said about that statement. I learned to serve the enemy notice that although his notice had been served, it would not under any circumstance prosper because God had already spoken His truth over my life.

I learned very early on that I could never match wits with the enemy. In all honesty, I never had to, because the Word of God says He would fight every battle for me, if I just stood still, and that in itself, was enough for me. Another valuable lesson I had to accept was that the only successful way the enemy could perform his trickery was through the body of another viable human being.

At first when I allowed my emotions to get in the way and speak on my behalf, I didn't like the aftermath of how I felt inside. I didn't like the temporary person I became in order to defend myself. And even in the midst of those conversations, I didn't like the words, tone or anger that rose up inside of me. At that moment, I was not fond of the person I pretended to be.

I wasn't a tough and rough person. I didn't even like to argue let along fight anyone. I thoroughly enjoyed reasoning and resolving issues not causing them or stirring the pot. How I often found myself around, near or even in the middle of those types of situations from time to time always left me puzzled and bewildered over the years.

So after high school, I thought, whew! I am free from all of the drama and childish ways of the people in school. I remembered thinking, after I graduated I am going to leave home to start a new chapter in my young adult life, and I am leaving the entire high school *"dramatization"* behind me. Yeah, right.

Little did I know or understood, I was simply approaching a new level of infancy. I mean, who knew such wars even existed? I certainly wasn't trained or even remotely prepared for the battle that was just up ahead in my life. Talk about an eye-opener. There were days, I simply had no words other than "Help me, dear Lord!"

In college, I was so green and sheltered as life goes. During all of my high school days, I had curfews and certain rules I had to follow while living at home with my parents. It was their house, their rules and their restrictions. To them, what they said meant everything, and there were no exceptions to their rule.

In college, it was obvious that I lived a sheltered life. The more experienced girls asked certain questions or made certain comments that I had no knowledge about. I was puzzled at best, and often I didn't feel it necessary to respond to their specific questions, or I didn't know exactly how to respond. I am not sure which made them angrier.

While it didn't make the other young women smarter or brighter than me, I knew by their various conversations that some or most of them were well experienced from the world standpoint. They were light years ahead of me per se in their viewpoints.

They guessed at most times based upon my non-verbal response, or slowness in responding to their questions, that I had not the slightest idea of how to answer their questions, let alone enquire about their personal motives at the outset. Most of the time I was simply not interested in chiming in.

I wasn't in tune enough in the Holy Spirit to ask whether I should even attempt to respond to their questions or whether I should simply chose to ignore their request. Sometimes I tried to fit in and play the part that I was as well versed in the conversation as they seemingly were.

Who was I kidding? They saw right through me as though they were looking through Swiss cheese. Realizing I would probably never fit in their tiny circle, I decided not to play their games. Instead, I moved forward with my studies and put my best foot forward. After all, I was the one paying for school, and there was no time to waste.

From time to time, other people may have thought I presented myself as a very proud or standoffish type of person. Some may have even thought I was the type of person who represented herself in such a way that made others around me feel uncomfortable or self-conscious about their own personal lifestyle. None of the above was true. I was just being me.

While I had no reason to compare myself to others, I knew in my heart I also had no reason to reinvent myself for the sake of others either just so they could become more comfortable with who they were around me. If anything, I spoke more loudly to myself that I had integrity and cared about building others up rather than trying to stick my foot in the pathway of others, causing them to stumble and fall for the appearance of looking taller. I never wanted to be a phony person, one who continuously smiled in the faces of others and stabbed them in their backs when they turned away.

I cannot honestly say how many countless years I spent worrying and wandering what is really going on in my life that is causing so much turmoil when it came to outsiders? I could not understand how that was possible when I spent approximately 65% of my time minding my own personal business and loving every moment of it.

I am one who never required a live audience in order to feel successful or important. I didn't require a tremendous amount of attention at any time from anyone. I didn't spend an incredible amount of time dating, and I didn't socialize a lot. I was fine with that, and I still am today.

However, I did like to dance, and laugh and smile a lot. Harmless—right? I thought so. So what was the meaning of all this extra stuff?

Now I am not saying everyone in the world was against me. It's just that for some, they thought I was entirely too straight-laced and perhaps too straightforward. And at times, I am sure the straight forward was probably the most accurate of them all.

Well, as time passed, nevertheless, God began to reveal to me that it was my light being revealed. Some weren't too excited about high beams being a reflector in the middle of darkness—especially when they didn't want to be seen or recognized by others at the moment. Unbeknownst to me, I was the driver in the car headed in their direction, absolutely clueless of my approach to them being the big reveal.

For example, sometimes in college settings, people approached me and asked if they could ask me a question about something important to them. My usual response was yes, and they did. However, after my response to their question, they didn't always like my biblical approach or response to their questions. Perhaps they thought I was putting them down for their beliefs or for how they approached the situation.

It was not always the case that my responses were not well received. Some appreciated my open-mindedness and thanked me for my honest response as opposed to simply agreeing with what I thought they wanted me to say.

Yet others did not receive the response well. Their actions and reactions in some cases roared their feelings. Their car tires screeched and a puff of smoke exploded out of the tailpipes, leaving me with the impression that perhaps my response was nothing they may have been looking for or necessarily wanted to here.

However, other times ended when I finished my response and the door simply slammed in my face. "Our" conversations stopped without a moment's notice. I guess they didn't like that response either—oh well.

Looking back on those times makes me laugh a little inside because eventually I realized responses like these examples are signs that this type of reaction is just a part of life. Not everyone is necessarily ready for truth. At other times, they do not necessarily care for whose mouth the truth is being spoken through. That has to be okay as well.

Over the years, these mixed emotions were beginning to take a toll on me. I knew that eventually I had to learn how to deal with rejections in the proper manner and not allow them to overtake me or take them to heart. I mean after all, not every rejection was a bad one.

Sometimes when I was in a crowd, I often found myself not responding at all because I didn't want to be considered as the odd person out or the one who differed from everyone else. It didn't mean I agreed with their views. I just didn't want to stir up trouble, so I kept my mouth closed and my thoughts to myself.

Still, I knew I had to find a way not to allow others to bully me because of my views. Nor should I allow others to control me in such a way my opinions or thoughts were not as respected as the next person. Needless to say, I had to pray a lot under pressure, whew!

I could not continue to allow others to regulate my thinking and responses for me whether they liked them or not. As I stated before, we are all very different individuals. We were not created to become clones in the world or space of another.

Over time, I found myself questioning why certain songs on the radio or buzzwords I heard through mere conversations often reminded me of something difficult in my life. Even after weeks, months and years later, things caused me to become sadden at a moment's notice. Those memories, at times, caused me to experience bouts of loneliness even when I had no real reason to be either.

There were even moments when certain responses from others took me emotionally to a certain place that was not always positive. If, heaven forbid, someone jokingly or not, blurted out something negative I did in my past 5, 10 or 15 years ago that bothered and embarrassed me. Especially if this was done while in the presence of others and everyone got a big laugh out of it to my expense.

Not only would I be challenged by this but I also realized I couldn't keep making excuses for this type of behavior from them or this type of reaction from myself. I had to confront the issues head on and find some sort of solace as to why or how come it existed. More importantly, why has it come back to haunt me from my past.

Either way, while they were busy teasing and taunting me for their own pleasure, I was hurting inside or experiencing rejection from their unending comments and remarks. I don't know if they knew it hurt me or if that knowledge would have made an impact or an indication to simply stop.

Yes, I understood I could have always blurted out something negative as well, and sometimes I did quite frankly. But doing so never made me feel good afterwards because that was not my real personality or mannerism. And I knew right off it wasn't the right thing to do. I almost always apologized right on the spot, which seemed to make me look like a weak person to them.

When I responded detrimentally, it was my way of finding an outlet so the negativity from them would stop at least momentarily. I could finally catch a break from it all. While I didn't always know how to handle conflict from a worldly viewpoint, I had enough of the Word of God in me that guided my responses and reactions.

Grounded with the fact that God would see me through what temporary giants I faced provided me with much strength and resolve at the time. Therefore, knowing the Word of God, for me, is what kept me out of making the latter of the choices set before me.

As I continue to grow in my faith, I often go back

and remember that scripture from years passed from the book of Philippians 3:13-14.

> *Brethren, I count not myself to have apprehended: but this one thing I do, forgetting those things which are behind, and reaching forth unto those things which are before, I press toward the mark for the prize of the high calling of God in Christ Jesus.* (KJV)

Slowly but surely I think, for some reason, I cannot shake the verse from my mind. Perhaps I need to revisit it again for my own peace of mind.

There it was again—those words pierced the very core of my being like a sharp spear. I knew I needed to do something upon reading those words, but I didn't know how or for that matter where to begin, so I began to pray and try to figure this thing out called *"true forgiveness."* I mean nothing else in my life was giving me the quality of relief I was desperately searching for and needing.

The thought of being able to leave my pain and unnecessary heartache behind and never having to relive those nasty harsh thoughts of what I had experienced over and over again was like receiving the gold at the end of the rainbow.

The notion of being able to let go of the entire let downs from others or the disappointments over the years sounded refreshing and like a breath of needed fresh air. I made up my mind. I was going after the true peace Jesus said I could have. And I was not going to stop until I personally experienced what I called true deliverance.

I was so busy trying to prove myself worthy to everyone else that I didn't realize I was more than enough for myself and others because of the price Jesus Christ already paid on my behalf at Calvary. I began to pay more attention to the present given to me, and less about what others thought of me.

I kept reading this scripture over and over again asking desperately, "Lord, how can I receive the strength and wisdom to receive true forgiveness. Tell me how do I do this? Is it really possible to do that? Will you grace me with this special gift?"

I wasn't interested in being happy—I was in pursuit of His total peace that surpassed all understanding.

And there it was again, *"forgetting those things which are behind, and reaching forth unto those things which are before, I press toward the mark for the prize of the high calling of God in Christ Jesus."*

Over time, I began to understand and embrace the fact that I actually had already received this gift when I received Jesus Christ into my life at the age of nine. What I didn't know was that I now needed to let go of the old way of thinking and responding and embrace this magnificent gift that already resided in me through the empowerment of the Holy Spirit.

I needed to allow the gift of forgiveness I had received from God to flow through me into the relinquishing of hurts and rejection. I need to allow His presence to flow through me and disallow the enemy to impart and input into my thinking and acknowledgement.

I knew that daily my mind needed to be re-filtered and renewed through the Word of God. I had to watch the way I now thought about things, and more importantly, what I was thinking and meditating on. In other words I needed to be careful about what I was thinking at all times.

I realized more and more that I needed the power of God to think correctly and godly. I had to learn how to pull down those continuous nagging low budget strongholds that tried daily to steal, rob and take away my God-given joy. I had to keep reminding myself that Jesus loved me. Having full acceptance of that love would render me victorious every time.

I knew that through the grace of God all things were indeed possible. I had to learn that grace *makes* and through my faith in God it allowed me to *take* on the presence of the Holy Spirit in my life. Through that forum, I could walk in the newness of the blood of Jesus to love my enemies and even my haters with the love of Jesus.

Chapter 4 – How Do You Let Go of The Past?

And the peace of God, which surpasses all understanding, will guard your hearts and your minds in Christ Jesus. Finally, brothers, whatever is true, whatever is honorable, whatever is right, whatever is pure, whatever is lovely, whatever is admirable — if anything is excellent or praiseworthy — think on these things. Whatever you have learned and received and heard from me, and seen in me, put these things into practice. And the God of peace will be with you.

Philippians 4:7-9 (BSB)

Letting go of our past is never going to be easy and convenient, no matter how hard we try within our might. In fact, letting go is not something we should attempt to do in our natural abilities. It was never designed to be. No matter how many times we practice standing in front of the mirror at home, it will never be accomplished without the help of the Almighty God.

Safe at home may provide some false sense of "security" in accomplishing this goal. Please be painfully aware, when we go out into public and have to face the real world again, we will find that our practicing techniques done at home behind closed doors is a whole different animal. At times, we may decide to remain at home where we believe we are safe.

In most cases when this takes place, we are often left to fend with our emotions all on our own. And, if we're not careful, the flashbacks of our old wounds come flooding in like a tidal wave of undealt issues with raw emotions attached. In that moment, we will not have a clue of how to react or respond differently.

I do not believe letting go of the past was ever designed to be necessarily easy. However, I do believe pain from our past is designed to show us an avenue in which to grow from them and a means to which we process things thrown at us differently. But only if we are willing to release and relieve ourselves of the past hurts and disappointments.

First, there must be a willingness within ourselves to want to let all the negativity of life go. Not for a while or for a mere moment, but we must really desire a true resolve within our minds and our emotions as a means to gain inward strength as we choose to forgive our offenders and then choose to forgive "ourselves."

Next, we must give ourselves permission to move forward and get on with our lives, leaving "all" of the mishaps, misunderstandings, misgivings, and entrapments behind. We can actually do that with God's strength and faith that all things are indeed possible with him who believes.

The absolute only way I believe letting go of our past can be done permanently is through the blood of Jesus and constant reliance upon His name. Even then, we have to desire to walk in His love daily. When we are tempted in our flesh to go back into our old methods and ways of responding or reacting, we have to say, *"I can do all things through Christ Jesus who strengthens me."* (Philippians 4:13) Then refuse to go back into the old mindset and be held prisoner by our old thoughts and ways of responding to negativity.

Letting go of a relationship, hurt, fear, past mistakes, sin, guilt, slander, anger, failures, regrets, worry, etc. is easier only when we realize God is in control. But He gives us free will and the ability if we choose to take hold of the one thing that provides us freedom.

We must be willing to recognize that He gives us the necessary tools along with His power to *forgive* and *live life*. While I am not saying it is always instantaneously done, it is a very positive and powerful start in the right direction when we make up our minds to move forward.

I have never seen anything positive come from a negative situation or relationship. Especially when both people involved in that relationship are relentless in their own fleshly pursuit to prove each other wrong and to always, always one-up the other in making sure the other is hurt and broken with no real chance of recovery.

In the end, if these two individuals only realized the

waste of spent negative energy, wasted time, waste of life and wasted words. They could have given life to that individual rather than defeat or death. Perhaps they would have valued and treasured those moments of time more wisely and used their words to build up rather than to tear down.

Instead of plotting, planning and lying awake at night allowing themselves to become infected and ill from drawing in the negative thinking and rehearsing how to plot *"successful revenge"* on the other into their mindsets, they could have enjoyed a peaceful night's sleep in the Master's arms.

I am sure if those individuals considered the enemy's tactics for a moment, they might have made a decision to choose different reactions. They could have chosen the option of not yielding themselves to the enemy plots of destruction. Knowing he uses them as channels through which his vile, venomous poisoning could be filtered through to harm and attempt to destroy the joy of another.

At that moment, this would have been a good place to stop. Repent. And think about the messages they were sending out rather than spend so much futile energy and time on getting their point across. When we consider what the Word of God has to say about things before resulting to our own underhanded means of doing business, it will save us a lot of unnecessary suffering, heartache and undue stress—not to mention backlash. After all, what we give out to others will eventually find its way back into our lives.

Let's look at Romans 12:16-18 in the Berean Study Bible, which talks about forgiveness.

The Power of Forgiveness

Live in harmony with one another. Do not be proud, but enjoy the company of the lowly. Do not be conceited. Do not repay anyone evil for evil. Carefully consider what is right in the eyes of everybody. If it is possible on your part, live at peace with everyone.

At this point, I can almost hear pages being ripped right out of my book from various readers going, "What? Who does she think she is telling me to forgive and forget and to move on?"

Well, I am someone who has lived with the regret of not doing it sooner. If I can reach out to others who have not made the decision to let it go yet, I plead with you to make every effort in trying harder.

Choosing to hold on to hatred, unforgiveness, hurts, wounds, etc., does not and will not add one strand of hair to your head. It won't help with your health, and it will not make you happy. So I say, please let it go, and do it sincerely from your heart. And then trust God for your healing, refusing to live the rest of your life holding on to negativity of any kind.

Holding on to our bitterness and unresolved issues only hurts us and causes breakdowns in our inmune systems where our health is concerned. According to an article that I read titled, "Unpack Your Emotional Baggage To Help Your Body Heal" by YourTango Experts, the author concludes while admittedly it is quite difficult to move forward and to forgive, it is imperative to know some of the effects worrying and stresses can lead to in our health.

Whether we are male or female, people in general who refuse to allow ourselves to be released from our emotional baggage is staggering in numbers. It is also suggested that many of our medical issues are often tied directly to our medical diagnoses. This is one of the main reasons one of the first questions our physicians ask when we become ill, is about our emotions .

The artcile goes on to say that often we are not feeling at our best self. Then it is vital to think back to what is tied to our emotions and our feelings at the time. In other words, are we sick as a result of the lost of employment, source of income, divorce, spouse passing away, friend betraying you and the list goes on and on. Some sickness such as rheumatoid arthritis may take several months before it can become symptomatic.

According to the article, there are other conditions or illnesses that can be reflected almost immediately such as:

- Constipation or diarrhea, as well as stomach pain/ulcers
- Back/Neck pain
- Depression
- Insomnia
- High blood pressure
- Anxiety/Depression
- Weight gain or loss (eating disorders always have an emotional aspect)
- Sexual problems

- Rheumatoid arthritis
- Fibromyalgia
- Asthma
- Cancers (for example, pancreatic cancer may present with depression before the patient is symptomatic with cancer)[4]

Another very important tool I learned in forgiveness and forgetting is choosing not to dwell on negative reactions from other individuals or negative things we have done to other people. When we understand we cannot control others, we should agree to pray for them that God will reveal Himself in a way they can receive the Lord into their lives. Neither should we attempt to be the spokesperson for those who choose to see the world through their own personal lenses or distractions.

No matter what, we still have to respect and treat those who choose to see the world as being a negative environment with no real purpose of existence with love and care as well. People who have never been introduced to the gospel according to the Word of God are cluesless that there is a better way to live their lives. And they won't know unless it is told and shown to them through our sharing, living and giving of ourselves to them.

Often when we encounter someone who doesn't know about Jesus Christ, they carry around with them a very small vision of how the world works. For most people, all they can see sometimes is that everything is

---

[4] (Experts, 2017)

doom and gloom. And what they see in the world today is all there is to it.

For others, they may have a small vision about themselves living a full life both here on earth and when they die and go to heaven. For them, it is all based upon their perspective and not the plan God has for their lives.

Therefore, it is virtually impossible for them to respond in a positive manner to anyone who is happy or excited about their personal journey while living in a world that everyday screams so much negativity in the news and other media. Every day some peole become extremely comfortable with where they are in life, even if it is the same place 20 years from now.

Based upon their views through the media and various social medias and their own personal perspective, there is very little, if anything, positive to hope for. For the most part, they can only see their lives from either being rich and successful or poor and struggling.

These types of individuals seem to get enjoyment from their negative views of how they see the world. Through their own personal lenses and negative words they use to describe their own personal lives, it may provide a sense of false power within themselves that this is just the way life really is for them.

One of the sad things about this type of behavior, if left unchanged, it will recruit other unsuspecting individuals who sometimes don't have a clue and are devoid and weak from the lack of reading and believing the Word of God for themselves into their web of anger, deceit and hurt as a part of their team.

Those of us who want more for our lives realize that when the enemy comes to flood our thinking with various negative thoughts and responses, we can choose through prayer and patience, to delete these nuances from our memory file. With the help of God as our mind regulator, we can choose to live freely through allowing the Word of God to retrain our thinking, which ultimately controls how we live our lives out loud. It is imperative, however, to make a conscious effort to play close attention to our thinking patterns and habits in making sure we don't return to our old way of thinking and living.

When we make a decision to never be found attempting to retrieve or restoring the old files (our old ways of thinking) from our memory bank by deleting the old negative thoughts and behaviors, we are in fact choosing to replace them with the sweet aroma of the Word of God for our daily living.

I remember one day while studying the word of God, a thought came to my mind. *"Brenda, you know you can choose to delete old files from your memory by clicking on the object or the thought, holding it with the mouse and dragging the thought to the delete folder of your mind. Then simply **release** the thought into the delete basket on your memory screen and let it go."*

Whether we are dealing or struggling with guilt, shame, embarassment, negatively speaking or listening to others speak ill of someone else, we can choose to come to a conclusion, Through Christ, we now have the power to simply let it go and never allow it to reign over our lives again. Praise God!

I am always amazed when I am engaged in various conversations and the words lead to, "I cannot stand so-in-so. They really rub me the wrong way. Just mentioning their names makes my blood boil."

I said, "Then change your way of thinking. Why are you spending so much time dwelling on them in the first place? The chances of them thinking about you in such a way or at all is probably nil."

The other thing I became mindful of was paying attention to what I was allowing my mind to dwell on. I noticed at various times throughout the day, I found myself drifting off into a wandering mindset about different things in my past. From various intervals during the day, and depending upon whether my thoughts were positive or negative, that lead my mood at the time.

Depending on the emotions attached to those thoughts, at times, I allowed the enemy to bring up those hurtful, useless things from the past. The enemy used them as an attempt to run roughshod over me and render me hopeless in those moments. If not careful, I found myself in that moment being carried away by my thoughts.

Because of my growing relationship with the Lord, I can tell I am much stronger, wiser and sensitive to His purpose for my life. Dispite the fact that trials happens daily, there is nothing more in this world I desire more than to please God with everything in me.

I am honored the Holy Spirit lives within me and on one

hand, He serves as a security system that alerts me before, during and when the enemy is in close range, attempting to cause me defeat. When this happens, I am alerted to cry out to God for help and He rescues me each and every time.

> *Whoever dwells in the shelter of the Most High will rest in the shadow of the Almighty. I will say of the* LORD, *"He is my refuge and my fortress, my God, in whom I trust." Surely, he will save you from the fowler's snare and from the deadly pestilence. He will cover you with his feathers, and under his wings, you will find refuge; his faithfulness will be your shield and rampart. You will not fear the terror of night, nor the arrow that flies by day, nor the pestilence that stalks in the darkness, nor the plague that destroys at midday. A thousand may fall at your side, ten thousand at your right hand, but it will not come near you.*
>
> Psalm 91:1-7 (NLT)

I am learning not to waste any time in rebuking the lies from the enemy and dismissing the enemies ill-fated intentions over my life. I absolutely refuse to be dragged or tricked back to the prison cell that once held my mind and heart hostage through my own thoughts being held captive in my thinking and living.

The moment I realized my thoughts were a repeat offence from the enemy, I began to take immediate control over that thought and pull down those strongholds in the name of Jesus. I began to pull down those negative thoughts that once held me captive by quoting the Word of God over each and every lie.

For instance, when the enemy came and said something negative about me or my spouse's health, I canceled that lie out by saying, "In the Name of Jesus, according to Psalm 118:16-18, *"The right hand of the LORD is exalted; The right hand of the LORD does valiantly. I will not die, but live, and tell of the works of the LORD. The LORD has disciplined me severely; But He has not given me over to death."* (NASB)

I destroyed the lie from its very root by allowing my mind to think on things healthy and whole from the Bible.

Choosing to let go and move forward is proving to be one of the best decisions I ever made in my life. Letting go of all the mental anguish, disappointments, negativity in my life and asking God to renew my mind daily and put a guard at my lips has proven to be a valuable asset to my daily living.

For me it was life changing and necessary to simply let it go and become determined to forgive others and ask God for strength to choose, thus empowered to take back the God-given authority to move on and upward with my life's purpose. Revisiting all of my old hurts, heartaches, guilt, animosities, stressful situations, disappointments and wounds from my past wore me out.

I came to terms through the Word of God that those old wounds were not adding one positive aspect to my life. In fact, they were stealing and robbing from my life. I recognized I allowed my negative thinking in some ways to determine my entire mood for the day.

Choosing to mediate upon right thinking, which is godly thinking, and letting go immediately of anything that wasn't God-centered thinking was one of the best decisions I could make. Choosing the peace of God is absolutely priceless, and that is a choice I willingly strive for all day each and every day.

I want to go on record by saying that having the peace of God in my life didn't come without decision making and true effort. Making time for some form of the Word of God every day must come through our efforts to either read the Word, listen to the Word, meditate upon the Word or praying through God's Word is what draws us closer to the peace of God. It will not come to us simply by running to God just in the time of real trouble.

During those lapsed moments in time when I literally gave over my authority to the enemy, I was drained mentally, physically, emotionally, financially, and spiritually. I was needlessly overwhelmed, burned out on trying to pretend those negatives thoughts, and sometimes negative people and things, were not interfering with my life.

Even though I rebuked, decreed and declared that no weapon forming itself against me was going to prosper; I had not noticed that some of those weapons were already forming against me. Most of the weapons were gunning for me at great rates of speed, I might add.

While I was busy rebuking at the front door of the problems, at times, I temporarily forgot I inadvertently overlooked that I had left the back door of my mindset wide open. I simply allowed the enemy to recapture those old negative thoughts and come in, bringing his partners of doubt and frustrations to steal my joy, peace and rest through that opened back door once again.

At times when I laid down at night to go to sleep, little did I realize I was merely doing so just in theory because my mind never truly shut off from the daily stresses and worries from the day. I felt as though some of the trappings of that day's stresses still rolled over and over in my head, as if I set the recorder during the day for a specific timeframe and recap or instant replay to begin at night.

Finally, through much prayer and consecration and really crying my heart out to God about wanting freedom in my thought life, I was able to receive the answered prayer I desperately needed. Through replacing a negative thought with God's positive Word each day, and most times throughout the day, I gained my freedom.

Through discipline and over time, I was able to share my heart openly with God about my fears of letting go of my past and the things and individuals who deliberately hurt me, mishandled me and overlooked me. I made a conscious decision to choose to rest totally in God alone. I knew if I wanted to enjoy the peace of God there wasn't another option. The enemy of our souls is relentless in his efforts and drive to trip us up and keep us bound.

The good news today is he cannot because those of us who are born again are saved and sealed by the blood of Jesus. We are in the hands of an Almighty God who will never leave us nor forsake us. It is one of God's greatest joys to lead and protect us and to provide all we need.

> *The Lord is my shepherd. I lack nothing. He makes me lie down in green pastures, he leads me beside quiet waters, he refreshes my soul. He guides me along the right paths for his name's sake. Even though I walk through the darkest valley, I will fear no evil, for you are with me; your rod and your staff, they comfort me. You prepare a table before me in the presence of my enemies. You anoint my head with oil; my cup overflows. Surely your goodness and love will follow me all the days of my life, and I will dwell in the house of the Lord forever.*

Psalm 23

At best, all the enemy can do is make vicious attempts to cause us to doubt the Word of God for our lives. He enjoys telling lies that God doesn't care about us and that He will not help us. Lie, lie, and more lies.

I have made up my mind that God is good. He is good all the time. He already paid my sin penalties upon the cross at Calvary. I am blood bought. I am redeemed. I am loved, and I am kept by the Almighty God! There is absolutely nothing the enemy can do to me that God does not see or cannot handle. The enemy is a defeated foe, and his days are numbered, praise God.

According to an article written by Daira Curran, May 2, 2014, she reflects this of what she describes in Psalm 23. I thought it was unique and wanted to share it with you.

THE

Within this passage, David only references the Lord as being His shepherd. He is emphasizing the word "THE" because He is well aware that there is no one else but God who can protect him from life's snares and pitfalls.

LORD

Next, David chooses the title for God Almighty as "LORD," which means master or owner. While David could have chosen many adjectives to describe the God he knew intimately, he chose to call Him Master.

IS

David didn't stop there. David continues by clearly communicating that THE one and only LORD, master and owner of his soul, IS. This word IS implies a present tense.

MY

The next word is MY, which is very personal. MY house, or MY children, implies it is yours to claim. The Lord was David's personal claim. This cannot come without a solid relationship. Yes, relationships go through highs and lows, but knowing that a relationship is yours, much like a marriage, can bring a sense of forever commitment which brings about true joy. Do you call Jesus yours?

SHEPHERD

David uses a word we often lack connection with, which is the word SHEPHERD. A shepherd has a responsibility and obligation to care for animals who would otherwise roam without guidance. We are the sheep. We can easily be led astray, and we need someone to direct us. David saw himself in this manner. Wouldn't you also admit this to be true in your own life?[5]

When this concept is first being embraced, it may appear that by resting in God we allow the enemy of this age to win the battle over us, and those who have hurt us to never receive what we think should have been their payback.

I thought by doing so, I was allowing the enemy to win, and that those who had hurt me would never receive reprimand for what they single-handedly did to me and my family over the years. It is very easy to want to see our accusers and enemies paid back for the pain they caused.

I had to come to grips with understanding. Unforgiveness, unresolved issues, hateful words, and unspoken forgiveness creates a spiritual prison called bondage for the person who desires to hang on to those collectible items and refuses to let them go.

The important things we must remember is that until we are willing to forgive and let go and move forward, it doesn't matter how successful we are. How many important people we surround ourselves with. Or how much money we may have in the bank. Our lives will always be controlled by the enemy until true deliverance from God is allowed to come in and flood our souls.

Sadly, some people have been emotionally and mentally locked up all of their childhood and well into

---

[5] (Curran, 2014)

adulthood because they hopelessly refuse to forgive and let go. They have been chained and bound for so long to the enemy's deceit that they have never given it much thought to living a godly free lifestyle.

Still, there are others who have been in their own private prisons for so long, even when the offended have forgiven them or they have forgotten the offense, the memories of it all still lingers on for many, many years thereafter. Sometimes, unbeknownst to the person who were offended.

When I allowed the Word of God to "minister" to me regarding forgiveness, what actually took place was being "cared" for and "treated and nursed" back into right standing fellowship with God.

I didn't know I was out of order and out of right standing with God. I was too busy focusing on my own hurts and wounds and tending to the need of what I thought was self-protection from the world. I didn't realize I could not supernaturally heal myself or take care of the matter by myself. I needed God to intervene into my life and help me.

It wasn't until I read in Vine's New Greek Testament Dictionary that the word "minister" denotes first, "one who discharges a public office at his own expense," then, in general, "a public servant, and minister." That's when the light bulb for my life and light in Christ literally came on in such a powerful eye-opening way.

You see, for the first time in my life, I realized whether the situation was hurtful, devastating, true or false, right or wrong, it didn't matter. Jesus Christ alone was the one who paid for my sins, shortcomings, mess-ups, wrong living, pride, mistakes... And it happened over 2,000 years ago.

He actually paid all the warrants for my arrest and my bail money. Thus, all the charges the enemy would go back through the files of my past, bring up, and attempt to use in a court of his law to convict me would simply be thrown out because he no longer had authority and power to do so.

That day, I came to grips that Jesus really and truly cares for me. It was there when I started searching the scriptures and really began to meditate upon the Word of God intentionally for myself.

I began to find true relief from the pain and disruptions in my life and realized no one else could "make me feel" a certain type of way. Only I could choose to take on that emotion by allowing the enemy to put me in a headlock if I didn't know any better or if I didn't know what the Word of God had to say about it.

The Word of God came alive in my thinking and handling of my daily living before God. I found the Word of God alone kept me in perfect peace with mankind, because it was no longer about them. It had more to do with me and how I saw people in general. And more importantly how I treated others.

Today, it is important how God sees me through carrying out His will and purpose for my life by how I serve and treat others. It doesn't matter how they may respond or treat me. I am only responsible for how I treat them.

Wow! What a daily challenge that is.

While I have not reach total perfection in this area yet, it is my heart desire to be mindful of my tone and responses to others—especially those who are not so gracious to me in their conversations or responses with me when we are engaged in dialogue.

During these times, I found myself searching for the peace of God that truly surpassed all of MY understanding. I hated the feeling I had when I was trapped in the web of others. It was sickening at best. I am the type of individual who needs space and room to live and thrive.

Today, I am mindful that the closer I am growing in Jesus Christ, the more peace of God I receive and am surrounded by his great grace in my life. Through the studying of God's Word, I find that His Word will actually guard my heart and mind. The negative accesses are not able to gain easy entry into my thought life and dominate my emotional rhythm like it did previously when I wasn't as watchful.

Daily, I began reading the Word for my own peace of mind and in doing so, I fully experienced the peace and very presence of God enter into my life instantly. From there, I longed to spend even more quality time alone with Him. I wanted to hear Him speak to me and share His thoughts towards me.

The more I aligned my will up with His words, I found I could think on those things that were true. I began to actually speak life rather than death over everything that concerned me and my household.

I craved the things that were honorable and right, pure, lovely and admirable. I decided to no longer allow myself to be around others who only saw the negative in other people, things or situations. I didn't want to associate myself with those who took delight in talking about and lying on others as a hobby. I decided to chase after the things that were of a lovely report. Those things that were admirable and excellent or praiseworthy unto God. I chose to think on those things because they made me smile both inside and out. And I know they pleased my Heavenly Father immensely.

When I carried out and acted upon those things out of an act of obedience in His name, it made Him smile. I didn't choose to do those things out of a sense of "duty" but because it was right for me to do personally—whether it was before others or not. I realized the Word of God directed "me" to carry out those things I had learned in both private and the public sector and within every possible aspect of my daily living.

I knew God wanted me to put those things I have heard and seen through His word into practice. Through those experiences and various practices, the peace of God will be with me and flow through me daily.

At first, it seemed impossible for me to wrap my brain around the possibility that God would allow me at times to encounter such negative stigma. Then, I realized God would allow and use these very things and people in my life to build me up in the long run. I realize the negativity wasn't there to hinder me but to grow me from the inside out. Let's face it, sometimes you never know what you would do or how you would respond to a certain situation until tried in it.

You may say, "I doubt that." But, I now know God would never cause me hurt in any manner. That's true. However, since the hurt and negativity were at that moment part of my life, God, through His word allowed me to know for myself how I could handle the situation. I learned by having the opportunity to keep my eyes on Him rather than attempt to fight the battle myself. The difference in the outcome depended very much on whose report I believed.

Oh at first, I was skeptical just like you, "God would never, ever do that. After all, He loves me too much for that, right?" Notice I didn't say God caused it; however, I did say God used that situation to build me up. Of course, I didn't see it that way then, but now I really can see clearer now that the rain is gone.

Through the Word of God I am able to see that we really can overcome evil with good—but only if we are more filled with the good as it pertains to the Word of God and not our flesh and our fleshy ways of handling things. You see, going to church is a beautiful thing. But going to church alone will not make you or me into the person of Christ we need to become.

Spending time alone with the Word of God through reading, praying and mediating is the only thing that truly bring us around and more interconnected to a closer walk with God. Through his word, we get to become linked up with His personality and see ourselves through His 3D lenses. We see how we should become disciplined enough to walk our lives out before him.

Through reading, searching, meditation and trusting God's Word for our lives, we begin to release our fears and angst. God is really in control over it all. He will fight and win every battle on our behalf if we are only willing to obey Him in the interim.

The more I learned about being at peace through the Word of God, the closer I came to knowing what God has in store for me was never in the past. In fact, it was just the opposite. Little did I realize, at that moment, He was preparing something much greater and exciting for my life. He had something much better than the relationship that wasn't working out for me anyway. He had something greater than my worries and my fears, God has a real plan.

He had a hope and a bright future for me. So why should I live in the dungeons of fear and dread, defeat and disparity? The more I humbled myself before God the more I understood. Therefore, it was becoming easier and easier for me to let it all go and focus upon what was ahead of me rather than continuously looking back at my past. Praise God!

It was a delight for me finding out daily that God has something greater than my past mistakes. When I trust in Him, stand strong in His word over my life, choose to let go of the negativity, and keep on moving forward to see what God has in store for me in my future, I will continue to witness blessings after blessings in my life. I learned to start getting excited about the endless possibilities and to get my hopes up while waiting for God to turn things around in my favor.

"For I know the plans I have for you," declares the LORD, *"plans to prosper you and not to harm you, plans to give you hope and a future."* Jeremiah 29:11 (NIV)

Section II: Trusting God No Matter What

Chapter 5 – Can Things Get Any Worse?

Put on the whole armor of God that you may be able to stand against the wiles of the devil; For we do not wrestle against flesh and blood, but against principalities, against powers, against the rulers of the darkness of this age, against spiritual hosts of wickedness in the heavenly places. Therefore take up the whole armor of God that you may be able to withstand in the evil day, and having done all, to stand.

Ephesians 6:11-13 (NKJV)

The thing I learned about growing is that you should never give yourself a dated estimated arrival time to stop officially growing or for learning more. As long as we exist in this world, we will have to fight spiritually to maintain for our lives what our God has already obtained through the dying of His Son, Jesus Christ, on the cross at Calvary on our behalf.

The devil is not going to lay dormant and allow us to have a carefree life in the Lord without coming after us fast and furious with everything he has in his weaponry. So what that means for us as believers is that we also need to bring our A-game to the cross as well. We must stand directly in faith that God has already taken care of everything we need on our behalf. All we need to do now is believe and stand in the faith of God.

How do we accomplish that? No other way than through the Word of God and the practice of living our lives out loud both privately and publically, leaning and depending upon the Almighty God. We must move in hot pursuit of the gospel of Jesus Christ above everything else.

So what that means is we cannot be walking around uncovered and basically spiritually naked as though the enemy cannot see, touch or even attempt to harm us from every conceivable angle. We must dress daily for spiritual success in mind. We cannot be seen in public or private with our spiritual armor all crooked and out of place—or, worse, locked up somewhere in the nearest cleaners to be serviced.

We shouldn't have our spiritual armor in the trunk of our cars or packed up in storage somewhere. Then, when the time of trouble arises, we cannot properly lay hold on it because we are unfamiliar as to where we left it last—or even being mindful as to when we actually last wore it.

Some treat their spiritual armor like everyday clothing. They take it off and hang it up in their private closets because they cannot possibly afford to be seen with it on twice in one week.

We must take special care to do our part in this battle called "life" if we are expecting to live victorious. Just because we fought a few bouts in the ring with the enemy over our peace and joy—and yes the enemy has been knocked out and counted down by the referee, Jesus Christ—does not mean the spiritual war is remotely over. Remember, as long as there is breath in our bodies, the enemy is going to launch his weaponry against us.

After all, one TKO does not qualify you and me as champions for life or champions of the right. We must continue to be vigilant fighters in Christ for our own private battles and coverings for our families, friends and love ones. Yes, God has indeed given us the victory, but we must always keep the trophy handy and in eye view to remind us how the victory was really won.

In fact, the Word informs us, "Put on the whole armor of God…" not bits and pieces. This isn't a fashion show or a new outfit where we experiment with various pieces. This is our life and well-being at stake, and we must take it all very seriously if we have a chance of standing strong and winning every time.

While some are spiritually content with winning every now and then, I am not. Because I have had enough close or tied fights, I am now in it to win it. Belt, title and even championship ring. I want it all! Take me higher, Jesus.

The armor of God contains various pieces: the belt of truth, the breastplate of righteousness, the "shoes" of the gospel of peace, the shield of faith, the helmet of salvation, and the sword of the Spirit. (Ephesians 6:10-18) It is important to know the various pieces. So if just one piece is missing, we know exactly what to look for through the absence of its importance.

These pieces have a description of what they are: helmet of salvation, shield of faith, loins girt with truth (belt of truth), and feet shod with the preparation of the gospel of peace (peace), the sword of the spirit/Word of God, and the breastplate of righteousness. The seventh is prayer. The helmet of salvation and the breastplate of righteousness also appear in Isaiah 59:17.

Unfortunately today, so many church folk walk around dressed to kill on the outside. Everything matches and flashes. Sadly, underneath those fancy and lavish outfits, they are missing the proper and necessary undergarments that help them to keep the victory before, during and after church services.

If any of these necessary pieces are missing, we should be able to readily tell. And it should not take us months or years to notice a missing link within our daily armor. We should be able to feel the noticeable void in our lives and daily walk with the Lord where victory is concerned almost immediately.

I promise you, if we have been use to wearing the armor of God, all of the pertinent pieces that make up its collection, when trouble starts, we would be able to tell the difference. When a piece of the armor is either missing or worn incorrectly, we know. For starters, the fiery darts from our enemies easily remind you and I what piece is missing based upon our response back to the enemy.

I believe we should never think about trying to out-perform the devil. He wrote the book on trickery and scheming. He can out lie us, out curse us, out scheme and connive us all in the same breath. He can even persuade us with wrong thinking if we yield to his faulty temptations.

Daily we must ask God to keep our minds stayed upon Him. We must ask God to please put a guard at our lips so we might not sin against Him. And lastly, we must be able to rightly divide God's truth and not be so quick to yield to the wiles of the enemy. Remember, he's had lots and lots of practice.

"For I know the thoughts that I think toward you, saith the LORD, thoughts of peace, and not of evil, to give you an expected end." Jeremiah 29:11 (KJV)

"Casting down imaginations, and every high thing that exalteth itself against the knowledge of God, and bringing into captivity every thought to the obedience of Christ." 2 Corinthians 10:5 (KJV)

As innocent as this statement may appear, it is everything but. In fact, if we only really knew how much control God gives us in the orchestration of our individual lives, some, if not all of us, just might faint—right there on the spot.

A lot of times, we are quick to blame God for the choices and decisions we made without ever considering Him in the beginning of our decision making. When those decisions we make turn out to be the worst decisions ever, we quickly ask, "God, why did you let this happen to me or my family or those that I love?"

Other times, we chant, "God if you love me, why didn't you stop me from doing this?" Never stopping to take into account our own actions, choices and mindset for the things we decided to do on our own.

We are quick sometimes to pretty much "tell" God what we have decided to do, and we just need His endorsement for payment, protection and provision of the whole thing. We don't necessarily need or desire His guidance and input in how our decisions will be handled—until of course, there is a snafu involved with the details. And then we need God to fix it right away.

We must be weary of the fact that when we choose to ignore God in all or any of the minute details of our lives, we can expect it not to go well, if at all. The truth of the matter is when we fail to invite God into our private spaces or what we may perceive as being our private spaces, in the end, we can only account for the remnants of what could have been so much better.

The point I am trying to make is we can only hold God accountable to us for the things we truly release to Him to handle. We cannot expect God to fight a battle for us that we never relinquished into His hands from the very beginning.

The excuses we may use as to why we didn't give it to Him are unimportant and pointless after the fact. The fact of the matter is, we didn't trust Him to handle it for us in the very beginning. Or if we did ask, we didn't believe He was going to answer us in time. We decided perhaps to look both ways and unquestionably move full speed ahead on our own. Therefore, we took matters into our own hands. And now what?

Daily when we turn on our televisions to the news,

Forgetting Former Things

within a couple of minutes thereafter, we can expect to encounter bouts of negative press. But we can also count on at least five to ten reports, fresh off the bat, being situations where someone made a decision where they never took into consideration the consequences or the outcome for their actions—such as stealing a car. Robbing a bank or murdering someone for her purse or other valuable items that didn't belong to them. Now, based upon their actions of sheer impulse, not only did their deeds cause the death or injury to another person, but also sometimes, the suspect will more often lose their own lives in the process.

These are such senseless situations and dangerous risks people take all day long—based upon "choices" never truly thought out—not really planned out with all the true possibilities of outcomes in mind at all.

Daily we make choices that could, and most often, alter the rest of our lives and the lives of countless of others with very little concern about what happens next. *"Casting down imaginations, and every high thing that exalteth itself against the knowledge of God, and bringing into captivity every thought to the obedience of Christ."* 2 Corinthians 10:5 (KJV)

Our thought life is very powerful and what we "think about and meditate on" constantly will come about eventually indeed, whether it is negative or positive. Some are not able to make the connection that their thought life and what they choose to meditate upon came back to haunt them.

Still they have no clue as to why certain things continuously happen to them. Not understanding that the idle mind really can sometimes become the devil's workshop, all because they invited the enemy in through their thought life. It's as simple and easy as that.

Back in the day when the Housewives of whatever city, first began airing, I began watching what I thought at first were just a couple of innocent episodes. I must admit, at first, I was interested in seeing more so I tuned in again the following weeks like clockwork. However, the more I watched, the more I found myself being drawn in by all the ridiculous and degrading drama.

Later on when the second season began to premier, I found myself being bothered by all the underhandedness and name calling, disrespectfulness and downright evilness blatantly displayed by the women on the show. They openly shared whatever they thought would bring about the greatest ratings for them along with the biggest payoff no matter the cost involved with little to no respect for themselves and apparently to no one else.

In just a short period, I could not stand to hear the music playing because I knew nothing good was going to come from watching another episode of these low-budgeted, disrespectful and no integrity television shows for an hour. I could have been spending time doing something of importance or helping someone that could benefit from a moment of my time.

Our lives turn out exactly in the directions in which we allow ourselves to be turned. We cannot give 20 minutes to the Word of God and eight-and-a-half hours

Forgetting Former Things

to the enemy, and think we are going to be substantiated for the long haul. Whatever we allow to influence our lives—whether it's gossip, backbiting, television or the Word of God—that's what is coming out of us in the long run. So we might want to choose wisely what we are adhering to.

I believe that every day, God votes for us. The enemy votes against us. But God gives us the wisdom, freedom, and ability to break the tie by choosing which direction we want to go in. That is why choices should never be made based upon emotions or when we are tired and weary. Most of the time, those decisions are made under duress and strictly flesh, knee-jerk reactions that can sometimes be made with very little truth and more fact.

Chapter 6 – Where Was God in All of My Suffering and Pain?

But now, thus says the LORD, your Creator, O Jacob, And He who formed you, O Israel, "Do not fear, for I have redeemed you; I have called you by name; you are Mine! When you pass through the waters, I will be with you; And through the rivers, they will not overflow you. When you walk through the fire, you will not be scorched, Nor will the flame burn you."

Isaiah 43:1-2 (NASB)

I want to begin this chapter off with some of my favorite very true, honest, and meaningful statements I have personally come to know for sure. As I continue to build and establish my relationship with the Lord, I am now able to attest to and affirm each of the statements for myself.

"God is Almighty, All knowing, more than Able, Greater than Great and quicker than quick. He absolutely can do anything but fail." I continuously find Him to be faithful beyond measure!

It is so easy for one to panic when trouble arises,

and "we notice" things are awry or are totally out of place in our lives. It is so easy for us to panic when the problem becomes noticeably too big for our handling.

It is also so easy for us to notice, when we cannot work things out on our own. Or when we feel the urge to throw in the towel or simply discard the towel altogether. Sometimes we may even feel it is not necessary to put wasted energy into throwing in the towel. Heck, why not just burn it, and say forget it all. Unfortunately, for some, that's the only time they will notice their thoughts, *"Hey. Wait a minute. Where is God in all of this?"*

The funny thing about all this is the fact that "God "never left. In fact, the mere fact you and I are still standing, proves He never, ever left. The real truth of the matter is we are really in trouble the moment our eyes opened this morning, before we got out of bed. But God!

In fact, when was the problem never too big? When were the bills not out of control? How would we get healed without God? How could we really withstand any test at all if it weren't absolutely, undeniably without the hands of the Almighty God resting over and in our lives?

You see, God has never left us. We are the ones who attempt to continuously go roaming off on our own personal scavenger hunts in foreign lands and situations without consulting the Lord at all. Let's face it. We try each and every day to keep some or most parts of our "private" lives private and out of the eye of God—as if we could.

So, the real question is not "where was God?" But rather, why did we ever think it was safe to wander off into foreign territories without God in the first place? Haven't we already been down this misguided, confused, dead-end street before? And haven't we noticed it always ends not in our favor one way or the other?

Once we accepted and acknowledged Jesus Christ according to John 3:16 *"For God loved the world so much that he gave his one and only Son, so that everyone who believes in him will not perish but have eternal life."* We must challenge ourselves to continue growing in and through His word for our personal lives from that moment forward. We shouldn't arbitrarily try to change the script because it doesn't suit our agenda.

As we *choose* to desire to learn and grow in his word daily is the only way we will certainly learn how to trust Him completely for everything. Not just when we are in trouble, but for everything. In other words, the more we learn of God, the more we can lean on and trust him for our personal daily care.

If we do not have time to read and study His Word, what we are actually saying is we don't have time to grow and build an intimate and personal relationship with Him. Therefore, we will be found trying to live our lives on our own recognition and terms when the Word of God is very clear about, *"Whoever wants to be my disciple must deny themselves and take up their cross daily and follow me.* (Luke 9:23 NIV)

Our God is and will always remain a very present help in our times of trouble and difficulties no matter how challenging, difficult and tiring our situations or circumstances become. When we choose to place our faith and total belief in God, we can be assured our God is always, always, and always a present help in our times of trouble. And when have we not been in trouble?

He will never abandon the ship. He will never skip town on us, He will never simply deny us or refuse to walk with us through whatever it may be. I am a personal witness that God will go before you and I, and He will make EVERY crooked path straight.

In fact, I not only guarantee it but I live by that mantra this very day. God loves us beyond our circumstances, conditions, situations and trials, especially when we move out ahead of Him and don't ask for His specific plan for our lives before we respond to his Word. The lack of our faith may wound him, but He still loves us.

A specific passage of scripture comes to mind even as I am writing this book. According to Ephesians 3:20-21 (NKJV) "Now to Him who is able to do <u>exceedingly abundantly above</u> all that we ask or think, *according to the power that works in us*, to Him *be* glory in the church by Christ Jesus to all generations, forever and ever. Amen." *Emphasis mine.*

I must share this revelation with you, because for the first time in all the other different times I have read this passage of scripture over the years, I failed numerous times to see this revelation. But thankfully today, dear God, I now see. Let's take a look.

Notice the scripture starts with "Now! To Him who

is able to do exceedingly…" We can see from the very beginning of this passage, nothing is hidden from its main purpose. Now! No delays, it's present tense. The scripture is readily opening our spiritual minds to understand that we must acknowledge God as the head of our lives at the outset—first and foremost.

Secondly--here it comes— we play a major role in the assurance we can become the recipients of those blessings when we continue reading "…*according to the power that works in us.*"

Wow! There it is. Right there in the open book for all to witness and to take ownership of for ourselves. The truth of the matter is that God is assuredly able to do exceedingly abundantly above all we ask or think of Him. And how is He going to accomplish that? Well, He will do it according to the power (*in other words, the trust, belief and the total dependence*) we relinquish to Him to accomplish through us.

Now before you rush in and say, "But I do trust God." I am not saying you don't on some level at least. But how about with *EVERYTHING* concerning you? You may say I don't know anyone who can truthfully say that. Well, here's the secret. You begin being the first one who sets that example.

In this day and time, we do not have the luxury of waiting on others to lead the way. We are the ones who must make that decision for ourselves. Trusting God with everything, for me, is the only way to live. It's not about being perfect or anywhere near perfect as it relates to "flawless." However, it does mean, at least to me, that I will make a committed decision to start today and move forward.

There again you might be saying, "Well, I don't know of anyone that trusts Him with everything. I mean, that seems virtually impossible." And I would say you are absolutely correct. Especially if the individual already made up his or her mind that no effort will be donated to the cause in the preparation of it all.

Our heavenly Father realizes and already knows what we can and what we cannot do without Him, which is absolutely NOTHING! That is a no brainer. However, He also knows those who desire, and even move pass desire, to acting upon relying on Him first without trying everything else or depending upon others first.

While God does not necessarily expect us to be "perfect," the old scapegoat word we always run back to—especially when we are not totally committed in the first place. He does expect to see effort from us with a sound decision to at least try.

The problem with that statement is we are not talking about everyone at the moment; we're talking about you—the one who is reading this statement as we speak. And more to the point, your situation to be exact. Why would you keep relying upon something or someone that has failed you too many times to put energy and effort into trying to recollect?

Through this passage of scripture, God is challenging us to see if we will be brutally honest with ourselves concerning our allegiance as trust goes in Him. You see, God has said through His Word to us, in the Book of Malachi 3:10 (HCSB) "Bring the full tenth into the storehouse so that there may be food in My house. Test Me in this way," says the LORD of Hosts. "See if I will not open the *floodgates* of heaven and pour out a blessing for *you* without measure or (until the blessing overflows." *Emphasis mine.*

To me, this verse says, "Brenda, it is not about your financial aspect of merely giving unto Me the 10%, but it is about your understanding of how much I love you and continuously watch over your *soul.* Nurturing you, counseling you, keeping you and sheltering you from each and every storm. Giving unto Me just proves to you that you can trust me in your entirety.

"That is the importance of the message here. I own all the silver and all the gold and everything that you have access to upon this earth. In fact, I own the earth as well and everything that dwells in it. I don't need, want or am depleted of anything. I ALONE AM GOD."

If it were simply because of money, as many people think, then it wouldn't matter the method in which the funds showed up at the church. In other words, one could stay home from church and *send* their tithe by whoever was going in the direction of the "church."

We could even pay the tithe by way of Internet services with the click of a button, or some other form of electronic means such as PayPal or a specific APP in our phones. We could even mail a check, for that matter.

I believe God is more interested in the quality of time we choose on our own to spend with Him. Of course He is the same God who wants to know about our problems, concerns and needs, but not because He doesn't already know about them. He still loves the fact we can come boldly to the throne and share our hearts without fear of judgement or condemnation.

This is different. I am talking about spending quality time with our Father without asking anything of Him. Just to spend that time "being" in his presence. Thanking him for **all that we are** and aware of what He has already done. And thanking Him for the things He is doing, as well as the things we are believing Him to do for us in the future. We praise Him for taking such great care of our every need.

We love on His name, His nature, His will and His awesomeness in our lives. We share the fact that He is Lord and we recognize, had it never been for Him, we never, ever could have remotely made it without Him at all.

While in His presence, telling Him, "You alone Lord" is our source and every incredible aspect of our lives. Oh how we thank You so much. You are the difference in our being able to enjoy life and peace on earth. We cannot live, move or have our being if it were not for You.

I believe the more time we spend in the presence of our Almighty God, we can't help but to get to know Him on a greater level. Monday – Saturday and by the time Sunday rolls around we are extremely excited and willfully cheerful about our giving in every way.

Imagine not having to be pumped and prodded to stand

and lift our hands in the sanctuary. Or to be prompted as if on cue to stand and "give God *praise*," as if we don't already have enough personal reasons to do so on our very own.

When we truly grasp that our Father loves us unconditionally, we won't be somewhere trying to make sure the check we write out for tithe will be the exact amount for 10%. Or trying to make the hard decision, stressing about whether we made the best decision in paying the tithe or the car note.

Because we have spent quality time with our Heavenly Father, who is in control of our livelihoods and the entire universe and everything that dwells in it, we can be assured we did make the right decision to always put God first, even when we are unsure.

So therefore, we don't bring our tithes begrudgingly to the alter with grim or worried looks on our faces—as though we don't know if we are making the right decision about paying our tithe due to there being a "lack" elsewhere if we choose to do so.

We should not bring our offerings out of distress so others will not think we don't give in church. Giving should be done purely out of love and our adoration for our Heavenly Father period. Giving should be done out of the sheer abundance of thanksgiving and gratefulness.

We should give cheerfully out of our livelihoods because now, having spent quality time in the presence of our Savior, we recognize who God is in our lives and the place He holds in our living and our giving. Without

God giving us His all, we would have absolutely nothing to offer Him including our money.

Yes. You guessed it. Because of the private set time we chose to spend in the presence of the Lord, we have now provided for Him a seat in the center of our hearts where only He reigns. There should never be another god of any type who reigns in that key position, but only the one true living God of all.

Having done so, now, when we come to bring our offering at the altar, on Sunday, we have gained a greater insight of who God is in our lives. And now we can feel free to relinquish ourselves more and more unto His will for us and be fully persuaded and confident that He hears us.

Our continuous fellowship with God being first place in our lives should put us more at ease that He will meet our every need, both seen and unseen. No matter what, because we give Him first place in our lives as Lord overall. Therefore, nothing is held back from Him during our worship or in our giving because He alone is our everything.

When we make spending quality time with the Lord priority and His relationship with us becomes *first place* and not just *commonplace* like all other relationships we have with everyone else, something deeper within our relationship with God happens.

> "When we put God first, he will always make sure that we are never last."
>
> Unknown

This type of relationship is being formed over time. We go from just being familiar with God by simply picking up the Bible, reading occasionally or recreationally, to seeking Him with our whole hearts just because we love Him. We find ourselves having a much deeper longing for His presence in our lives.

God knows the more deliberate desired time we choose to spend with Him, just for the sake of becoming closer to Him in our devotion to know Him better automatically renews and rekindles our love and trust being established. We reach the point where our giving of both tithe and offering would not become a cumbersome strain, struggle, worry or fear.

In fact, we probably gain a greater knowledge and assurance that God is far more concerned with blessing us through our giving than we are mindful of Him desperately wanting to bless us through our giving.

The more we learn about the love God has for us, the provisions He alone provides daily, the fact He is the One who takes care of us period. The more we should want to give back. Until we fully get it that our stability does not come from any other source at all, but Jesus and Him only, we will always give beneath our greatest potential.

Our main source of survival and livelihood can only come from God and nothing or no one else. In fact, it is not even possible. Because in the beginning, He, God made and created both the heavens and the earth and everything that is made in it. That means not only you and me, but every possible source as well. You see, if it's good, God made it.

Therefore, we cannot, nor should we, ever rely upon our employers, not our careers, not our Social Security checks, nor our retirement funding, 401ks nor any other temporary method for our means of livelihood. We certainly cannot depend upon our investments or even monies someone deeded to us through a will, trust or otherwise. God alone is our only reliable source.

All life and divine protection comes directly and strictly from God himself. He alone is our strength, our way, our hope, our provider and our every need-meter in the entire earth. There is absolutely nothing we can do, or will ever do in this world, without Him. Apart from God's hand being over our lives, we can do nothing at all.

So, Malachi 3:10 doesn't stop with us bringing the first tithe into the store house, but continues by saying in the next couple of verses "...See if I will not open the floodgates of heaven and pour out a blessing for you without measure or (until the blessing overflows) *Emphasis mine*.

In other words, what I believe God is saying is, "The first thing I am going to do is shower you with my immeasurable blessings, because of your obedience to Me and your understanding of how much I love you first and foremost.

"The fact you are mature enough through the word to know that when you consider how much I love you, there should be no momentary value placed upon your giving back to Me, let alone hesitation of giving at all."

This promise is made to the person who obeys God by putting Him first before the bill collector's paid, before the student loans are paid, or going out to dinner, and shopping sprees or what-have-you are done. Putting God first shouts volumes. "Lord, I trust you above all to take care of me and every single need I have in my life."

In verse 11, the scripture makes this commitment. "'Then I will rebuke the devourer for you, so that it will not destroy the fruits of the ground; nor will your vine in the field cast its grapes,' says the LORD of hosts." To rebuke, according to Bing Dictionary, means to reprove, reprimand, chide criticize adversely, and intent to correct.

The scripture is saying that whatever battles I had to fight on my own, He, God, will fight for me in a greater measure when I put Him first. Yes, I still have to pay those whom I owe. But God will make sure creditors I owe will treat me fairly and above board.

He will make sure the enemies of this world don't take full advantage of me financially, spiritually, mentally or emotionally. In other words, He will give me wisdom in all things, so whatever dealings I have will work out for my good.

Are you ready for this? Here comes the third blessing and promise to us. In verse 12, He says, "'All the nations will call you blessed, for you shall be a delightful land,' says the LORD of hosts." Okay, okay, I'm getting a little too excited here and ahead of myself, but if I don't say this now, I am probably going to spiritually explode in the third promise made to us in this chapter.

If we will just learn how to totally relinquish, rest, trust, believe in God first and foremost, those who once looked down their noses at you and I—because they deemed us to be pitiful, downtrodden, never moving forward or always living in the land called lack—are going to be in for a shock when they see what happens. God propels us light years ahead in everything that concerns us all because of our obedience and His favor upon our lives. Praise God!

The more we learn about God, the more we find our God is generous in His mercy and great grace towards us. He is Almighty. He is a very present help when we are in trouble. Remember—when are we not in trouble? He is the Source, the Keeper and the Purpose for our very existence. God cannot lie. He is the Alpha and the Omega, and He will complete whatever it is He has started within us for His glory alone.

Unfortunately, for some, the only time God will have their attention is during what they consider a crisis too large for them to take personal ownership of. For most, by the time the problem is temporarily surrendered to God, they are exhausted from trying out other whimsical measures to try and fix the problem or the circumstance on their own.

Even after sermons have been preached to surrender everything unto the Lord, or classes have been taught about surrendering everything to God, there will still remain some who will still say, "No, thanks. I got this."

Still, for others when they feel God has not come

through for them as quickly as they would like, they will become frustrated and sometimes doubtful that God is even interested in hearing their prayers. And if that is their assumption, they may even turn away from God and possibly leave the church even if it is temporary.

Even at times when I became frustrated and irritated because one, or several of my prayers, didn't get a quick turnaround response to my likening, I am sure I felt some type of way that perhaps God was never obligated to bless my disobedience or lack of faith. But He does promise to bless me when I know, trust and stand on His Word.

> *The LORD is good, A stronghold in the day of trouble, And He knows those who take refuge in Him. But with an overflowing flood He will make a complete end of its site, and will pursue His enemies into darkness.*
>
> Nahum 1:7-8 (NASB)

Our God is a God of order. He expects us to know His Word, know Him and to live our lives according to His Word. While He understands we are not "perfect human beings," (*living a flawless lifestyle*) He also understands that He placed within us the ability to make intelligent decisions and to use our God-given abilities to choose right from wrong.

So when we deliberately or unintentionally choose to make our own way without guidance or help from

Him, we soon find out our efforts to lean and run to God after the mess we've created will sometimes be met with our own disappointment. Because we failed to recognize that yes, God will deliver us. However, the consequences from our decisions are left for us to deal with.

And when some realize that, they will lash out at God or become depressed, doubtful and unmoved about what the Bible has to say about their situation. They inevitably turn away from God in their anger or disappointment of how they felt God chose to respond to their situation, failing to realize God never left them at all.

I mean who wouldn't want to live a stress-free, uneventful life, free from every conceivable trial, problem or worry. Who wouldn't like to have all the financial security one could only dream or imagine.

Since God is the source of all goodness, it would also be fair to say His glory is the wellspring of all joy. What God does for His own sake benefits us. Therefore, whatever glorifies Him is good for us, and sometimes that may include enduring bouts of sickness or other testing.

I know many of us, me included, do not enjoy any time sickness attaches itself to our bodies. But the fact is, sometimes, as Christians, we do suffer with various trials that may include suffering God allows into our lives.

Even though many of us hate the mere fact of any type of suffering, it is important to understand God refines us in our suffering and graciously explains why. *"See, I have refined you, though not as silver; I have tested you in the furnace of affliction. For my own sake, for my own sake, I do this."* Isaiah 48:10

(NIV)

It is imperative we get a solid understanding that the universe is about God and His glory—and whatever exalts God's glory works for our ultimate good also. That does not mean God is mean or hardcore in any shape or manner. It just means, no matter what comes our way, whether we deem it right or wrong, just or unjust, we can be assured if it is God's perfect will for our lives, He will get the glory. And we will ultimately have the victory!

Believe it or not, it has been while I experienced what I called *"great suffering"* at the time—when I felt my lowest point in that moment—I know beyond a shadow of a doubt, I grew and matured in Christ the most. Because in that moment, I sought after the will of God for my life more and with a greater vitality level of hunger and thirst.

I spent more quality and reserved time with God. More than I was averaging prior to the trial. I sought after Him, and I went after His presence like nobody's business. Why? Because I had to get to know Him deeper and more surreal in my life for myself, if I had even the slightest chance of making it through that torrential storm successfully.

What I found was the more time I spent making a "decision" to come into the presence of God, the more I learned about Him and how much He cared about my well-being. I discovered how much He really loved me and desired the best for me at all times. I learned there was absolutely no place I could hide, run or move out from under the scope of God. He was indeed an ever-present presence in my life.

It is said there was a gentleman by the name of Josef Tson, who faced much evil in communist Romania. He was quoted as saying, *"This world, with all its evil, is God's deliberately chosen environment for people to grow in their characters. The character and trustworthiness we form here, we take with us there, to Heaven."*

The book of Romans and 1 Peter 4:19 makes it clear that suffering is a grace from God. It is a grace given us now to prepare us for living forever. Without growing in Christ most of us would easily desire to take the easy way out of hard things. However, in the end, how would we really know what it means to endure and to rely and trust God in all things? If every time we got into trouble or a difficult situation, He bailed us out in an instance, how would we learn?

In order to really know if we can lean on and trust God with His Word, our character and integrity must be built and tested. Not for the Word's sake, but for the sake of the Word in our lives and our true in-depth understanding of what it means personally to rely and lean on God to bring us completely through every situation.

If God wanted to, He could simply create whatever He wanted in order to carry out His purpose completely upon earth—such as rocket scientists, mathematicians, athletes, and musicians at the outset.

He doesn't. Instead, He chooses to create individuals who will take on those roles. Over a long process of time, they took various training and test skills to develop their personal expertise to accomplish the joy of becoming an expert in those specific fields of work. Why? Because we learn to excel by handling failure properly. Only in cultivating discipline, endurance, and patience do we find satisfaction and reward in our respective crafts.

When we think of the word "love," we immediately believe it means to "do no harm." It really means, *"to be willing to do short-term harm for a redemptive purpose."* A physician who re-breaks an arm or a leg of his patient in order for it to heal properly harms his patient in order to heal him.

In his book, *A Grief Observed*, C.S. Lewis wrote, "But suppose that what you are up against is a surgeon whose intentions are wholly good. The kinder and more conscientious he is, the more inexorably he will go on cutting. If he yielded to your entreaties, if he stopped before the operation was complete, all the pain up to that point would have been useless. … What do people mean when they say "I am not afraid of God because I know He is good"? Have they never even been to a dentist?"[6]

If cancer, paralysis or a car accident prompts us to draw on God's strength to become more conformed to Christ, then regardless of the human, demonic, or natural forces involved, God will be glorified in it. When I was going through a very challenging time in my life, I really came to understand that God's definition of a particular word or phrase is a different definition than

---

[6] (Lewis, 1963)

mine.

For example, He does work all things for my eternal good and His eternal glory. But his definition of good is different than mine. My "good" would never include cancer or witnessing a young widow grieving over the loss of her spouse. My "good" would include only complete healing all the time, and no one would ever experience dying or death.

However, God does not cause bad things to happen to us, I realize today, because God is an all-knowing and all wise God, He knows no matter the sufferings, in the end, it will all work out for our good and His glory. Because those of us who are born again will never be separated from His presence, we will live with Him in eternity forever.

No one has a complete true pulse on why certain pains and heartaches happen in life. And though I believe we can ask God why, it is important to note—we need to be aware it is up to God's discretion whether He chooses to answer us in that regard.

And even if He chooses to do so, I am not sure the answer would truly be enough to pacify us in our pain and heartache. Because we are in this human body, it is, in my opinion, impossible to comprehend such an undertaking as it relates to the will and purpose of God at our weak and limited levels. We can rest, however, in the fact God can use suffering to display His work in you and me.

When Christ's disciples asked whose sin lay behind a man born blind, Jesus said, *"Neither this man nor his parents sinned…"* John 9:3 (NIV) Jesus then redirected his disciples from thinking about the *"cause"* of the man's disability to considering the *"purpose"* for it.

He said, "This happened *so that* the work of God might be displayed in his life."

A gentleman by the name of Eugene Peterson paraphrases Christ's words this way. *"You're asking the wrong question. You're looking for someone to blame. There is no such cause-effect here. Look instead for what God can do."* John 9:3 (MSG)

Nick Vujicic entered this world without arms or legs. As told in his life story on his website, www.lifewithout limbs.org, both his mom and dad, an Australian pastor, felt devastated by their firstborn son's condition. "If God is a God of love," they said, "then why would He let something like this happen, and especially to two committed Christians?" But they chose to trust God despite their questions.

Nick struggled at school where other students bullied and rejected him. "At that stage in my childhood," he said, "I could understand His love to a point. But … I still got hung up on the fact that if God really loved me, why did He make me like this? I wondered if I'd done something wrong and began to feel certain that this must be true."

Thoughts of suicide plagued Nick until one day the fifteen-year-old read the story in John 9 about the man born blind. "…but that the works of God should be revealed in him." (NKJV) He surrendered his life to Christ. By age twenty-six, he earned a bachelor's degree and now encourages others as a motivational speaker.

"Due to the emotional struggles I had experienced with bullying, self-esteem and loneliness," Nick says, "God began to instill a passion of sharing my story and experiences to help others cope with whatever challenge they might have in their lives. Turning my struggles into something that would glorify God and bless others, I realized my purpose!"

I can personally testify, as Nick did so wonderfully with his story. As I continue to seek after Christ for a closer walk, through the word of God, I came to believe the Lord was going to use me to encourage and inspire others to live to their fullest potential and not let anything get in the way of accomplishing their hopes and dreams. And to date, I am fulfilling that lifelong dream.

As God's purpose became clearer to me. Now I'm fully convinced, and I understand His glory is revealed as He uses me just the way I am. And even more wonderful, He can use me in ways others can't be used for His expressed glory.

In the process of God making and carving us into His perfect image for our individual lives, it is often viewed as challenging, trying, and difficult to continue hanging in there, because we don't understand the necessary process.

Like sheep, we don't possess the necessary patience and stamina to wait on God and choose to believe He is always working things out for our good and His eternal glory. So we worry, doubt, fret and even moan and groan during the process of change.

Most of the time, while we are wondering where is God and what is He up to in our lives, we are not always cooperating with Him. Most of the time we can be found like little children, squirming in our chairs, complaining and murmuring and asking, "Lord, just how much longer?" "Are we there yet?" We don't like to wait on anything. We want instant gratification, even when there is no understanding behind it.

In our minds, we think we are totally cooperating with God when in fact, God has called us to yield ourselves by submitting to his molding of our lives. Because we fail to see the person God intends to form through our adversity, we too may resent any type of chiseling away of the old man period.

Sometimes, we willingly may settle for some remains of the old man at any cost, even if it is just a few slithers. We must remember, the Master Artist chose us, when we were flawed and unusable, to be crafted into the image of Christ to fulfill our destiny in displaying Jesus to the watching universe.

No matter what, it is never easy to endure hardship especially for periods of long-lasting trials and difficulty. I don't know about anyone else, but when enduring hardship it seems as though Satan will bring every conceivable hardship possible in our direction, designed to keep us away from victory in Christ.

And when we ask God to remove the chisel because it hurts, God doesn't because He knows it's a means of transformation. "And we, who with unveiled faces all reflect the Lord's glory, are being ***transformed*** into his likeness with ever-increasing glory." 2 Corinthians 3:18 (NIV)

In her book, *When God Weeps,* Joni Erickson Tada writes, "Before my paralysis, my hands reached for a lot of wrong things, and my feet took me into some bad places. After my paralysis, tempting choices were scaled down considerably. My particular affliction is divinely hand-tailored expressly for me. Nobody has to suffer 'transverse spinal lesion at the fourth-fifth cervical' exactly as I did to be conformed to His image."[7]

God uses suffering to purge sin from our lives, strengthen our commitment to Him, force us to depend on His grace, bind us together with other believers, produce discernment, foster sensitivity, discipline our minds, impart wisdom, stretch our hope, cause us to know Christ better, make us long for truth, lead us to repentance of sin, teach us to give thanks in times of sorrow, increase our faith and strengthen our character.

And once He accomplishes such great things, often we can see that our suffering has been worth it. God doesn't simply want us to *feel* good. He wants us to *be* good; and very often the road to *being* good involves not *feeling* good. *Adapted from If God Is Good by Randy Alcorn.*[8]

---

[7] (Tada, 2000)
[8] (Alcorn, 2009)

Chapter 7 – Now, What Do I Do?

If any of you lack wisdom, let him ask of God, that giveth to all men liberally, and upbraideth not; and it shall be given him.

James 1:5 (KJV)

That's a good question and also one that deserves a well-thought out response. I am sure you agree that sometimes, there just doesn't appear to be a solid answer—at least not one that calms all of our fears and doubts when trouble and/or uncertainties arise seemingly out of thin air. Now what? What do we do with such little to no notice? Should we move forward, proceed with caution on our own or what?

Fortunately for believers, we don't have to search blindly in the dark all on our own. We have a loving, gentle and all-knowing Savior that is more than willing to lead, guide and direct us through it all, if we only ask, believe and receive from Him. In Isaiah 55:6, the Word of God says, "Seek the LORD while he may be found; call upon him while he is near." (NIV)

God doesn't want us trying to figure things out without Him and His guidance in our lives. He desires us to ask for His wisdom and expertise about all matters. There is absolutely nothing too small or too large He does not want to be involved in.

You may be saying, "Well Brenda, if that is true, if God knows everything, why do I need to still ask?" My honest response would be to inquire of His help in your life for the direction "you" need. You see, it isn't enough just to ask and still continue to do what I want. Instead, we must ask with sincerity of heart, get an understanding and then follow suit after the leading of His answer.

In addition, the Word of God continues by expressing to us that it doesn't matter when we cry, how we cry, how long even we cry unto Him. He promises not only to hear us, but also to respond to our pleas.

Psalms 34:17 says, "When the righteous cry for help, the LORD hears and delivers them out of all of their troubles." The problem is we have to learn how to hear, take and believe. We have received the direction, answer and response we need.

God wants to grow us in faith and teach us we can move forward from any difficulty, tragedy, hardship and pain when we put our total reliance in His name and His ability. 2 Corinthian 9:8 tell us, "And God is able to make all grace abound to you, so that having all sufficiency in all things at all times, you may abound in every good work."

When we come to understand that God has delivered us from the domain of darkness and transferred us to the kingdom of His beloved Son, we can trust in the LORD with all of our heart, and not lean on our own understanding. We will be able to acknowledge the Lord and know He will make straight our paths.

Because our God is able to make all grace abound to us, having all sufficiency in all things at all times, we may abound in every good work.

So what do we do next?

We lean in hard and pay attention to what the Word of God is saying to us. And we learn how to trust God in and for all things, at all times.

"He has delivered us from the domain of darkness and transferred us to the kingdom of his beloved Son." Colossians 1:13 (ESV)

"Trust in the LORD with all your heart, and do not lean on your own understanding. In all your ways acknowledge him, and he will make straight your paths." Proverbs 3:5-6 (ESV)

"And God is able to make all grace abound to you, so that having all sufficiency in all things at all times, you may abound in every good work." 2 Corinthians 9:8 (ESV)

Chapter 8 – Is Forgiveness Necessary?

"For if ye forgive men their trespasses, your heavenly Father will also forgive you."

Matthew 6:14 (KJV)

Have you ever been deceived? Wounded by someone you thought you could trust with your deepest secrets? Have you ever believed in someone who didn't necessarily believe in you?

Have you ever held out for something very important to you, only to find out it was never going to arrive, and no one ever told you? Did you ever fall in love and really believed it would be always and forever, only to find out your plans were not necessarily their plans?

Well the list could probably go on for centuries and still not cover all the basis of hurt, deceit, anger, ill will, deception, hatred, disappointments, discouragements and failures.

In fact, the mere mentioning of someone's name can set

us back at least two years and counting, even though the particular incident or situation happened countless hours, weeks, months or even years ago.

For some, it doesn't matter how long ago the hurt or the disappointment happened. To them, because the tape in their mind is designed to play continuously, the heartache of it all remains as fresh today as if it took place a few precious moments ago. And to that individual, he or she cannot seem to let it go or move forward passed it.

On one hand, it is too difficult to re-live they think. On the other hand, it is even more painful and difficult to remotely let it go. Fear may drive our thinking—perhaps if I do so, I will be allowing the other person to get away free of charge or without paying the "*subliminal*" price of hurting me. Especially true if the other person "appears" to have moved on with their lives, careers, marriages, friendships etc.

Have you ever been out on the town or someplace fun enjoying yourself and having a great time when all of a sudden, he or she showed up? Unbeknownst to you, they were invited to the same event. Within a matter of seconds, it seemed all of the joy was suddenly sucked out of the room because of their presence.

What I realize now more than ever is the things that may have been said or done towards me were difficult to handle or accept. I didn't know at the time I didn't have to accept those things into my personal vortex and take them on as though any of that negativity were acceptable or even true in the first place.

I honestly did not know I didn't even have to be offended unless I chose to be. What do I mean by that statement?

Well, I now know when mean and ugly things are hurled out in the atmosphere towards me, those curt words or comments were designed by the enemy to break, hurt, kill or steal my joy. I don't have to wear it as a personal garment designed for my outlook. Why? Because "I AM AN OVERCOMER" in Christ Jesus, and I know it.

I can either choose to not even open my mouth and "partake" of such nonsense thus allowing the enemy to remotely think he can and will interrupt my day; let alone steal my joy. If I choose to say something, I can say what the Word of God has said about me over 2,000 years ago. Either way, it's my choice and doesn't have to be proven or accepted by anyone else, because I know I already have the victory in Jesus Christ's Mighty Name!

So is forgiveness necessary? Absolutely it is. In my world, it is not an option. It is a must, because forgiveness is my personal get out of jail card for me to remain in freedom from guilt and condemnation.

Through my forgiveness to others, it affords me the continual liberty to move about the earth in the peace, joy, and godly wholeness I need to thrive, without being pulled down by unnecessary weight and condemnation by this world and people.

When I choose to forgive others, it is a release form I spiritually sign that says, *"Father, in your Name, I choose to forgive those individuals who perhaps meant it for evil or intentionally for my worst. But through your mindfulness of me and your perfect will for my life, you interrupted Satan's program and ill plottedness along with his wicked devices. You made it all for my good and for that, Master, I am eternally grateful.*

And the way I express to you my gratitude is by immediately coming into agreement with you. I choose to release those individuals from the retaliation of hurt, harm or danger coming from my own desires to see them hurt in any manner. In Jesus Name, I thank you, and I believe it's already done!"

Another thought I had towards forgiveness is it is a personal decision. It is something made without the other's consent and or approval. After all, it is your heart that must stand pure before the Almighty God. It is your conscience that must be cleared from all unnecessary debris and clutter of this world so you may receive ALL God has for you.

Sometimes you spend too much time getting the opinions and thoughts from others, who may or may not have any direct or immediate benefit from your pain, hurt or unforgiveness residing in you. Only you can set yourself free from that damage control. And in that instance, you and I must seek the face of God for ourselves and ask Him for the much needed strength, wisdom, and guidance about how we should proceed.

The danger in asking others is that the majority of the time, you may run the risk in only getting their fleshly response such as, "If I were you, I wouldn't have anything else to do with them." Or, "forget about them, they did you wrong first." Though any of those comments could hold at least five percent of leverage, any of that decision making will block your blessings from being received if truly left undealt with as it relates to unforgiveness.

Forgiveness is vital to the person holding the grudge because if unforgiveness continues to reside within a person, it will inevitably cause important and necessary things concerning their personal journey to be blocked. And that person will never, ever reach his or her greatest potential God alone intended.

Remember, forgiveness is never about merely mouthing the words, knowing our hearts are still in anger management and hateful territory. It is a matter of the heart. I have heard this statement more than once, "I may forgive, but you better believe I'll never forget what they did to me." Well, in my opinion, you are still in the same place you were before.

Forgiveness to me is about giving myself permission to let go of all the old pollution, stagnate things that keep me bloated with unnecessary chemicals and waste that hinders my personal growth. I am not letting someone else off the hook. I am taking myself off the ventilator and allowing myself to move forward in the will and direct purpose of God for my life.

I am refusing to allow myself to die quietly or suffer in silence while the other people have the best time of their lives, seemingly at my expense and their makeshift control. The devil and his entire army is a liar and the truth is not in them. Choosing to forgive others is the ultimate benefit to maintaining peace in my life through what Jesus Christ has already obtained for me on the cross at Calvary.

Choosing to forgive is powerful, and it is in itself a very powerful, precious tool to have within our repertoire. While forgiveness is not the easiest conversation to have with others, it is a process that can be achieved, especially when our minds are made up, and we are in agreement with God to do so.

"For if ye forgive men their trespasses, your heavenly Father will also forgive you." Matthew 6:14 (KJV)

Another way to look at unforgiveness is holding on to things that are no longer beneficial or serve your real purpose. Things contrary to the plans God has for your life should never be held on to or used as a weight or a millstone around our necks, which we proudly wear as a precious gem or beautiful necklace.

There ain't anything pretty or helpful about a brick or a humongous stone binding, chocking the life right out of me or hindering appropriate movement in my life. In fact, John 10:10 makes it very clear when it says, *"The thief comes only to steal and kill and destroy; I have come that they may have life, and have it to the full."* (NIV)

To allow anything to interrupt the perfect flow of Jesus Christ in our lives would be to merely make room for detraction and distraction from our real purpose.

Another important aspect about forgiveness is asking God to help us clear up any misunderstandings, misconceptions, misgivings and negative aftermaths once the olive branch of true forgiveness has been extended.

Sometimes, even when asked for forgiveness or we forgive others, it is important to note the other party may not be willing to accept the olive branch at that point. However, as long as the genuineness on our part is authentic, we must be willing to allow the love of God to fill that previous place of bitterness and deny its temporary reign over our lives. Then, we choose to press forward with our lives and the love of Jesus ruling forever.

Section III: The Choice to Move Forward

Chapter 9 – What Was the Purpose of the Pain?

"I consider that our present sufferings are not worth comparing with the glory that will be revealed in us."

Romans 8:18 (NIV)

Recently I read an incredible article by Gavin Ortlund titled "A Deeper Look at What the Bible says about Pain and Suffering." Interestingly enough, the article shared a lot of thought provoking concerns as it relates to suffering in the Bible.

To begin with, Mr. Ortlund stated, *"The Bible is deeply sensitive to the problem of suffering, including the internal suffering that many modern people face. It has something to say to us about these issues, if we have eyes willing to read it and ears willing to hear it."*

Further, Mr. Ortlund continues to elaborate on what he calls, "The Seriousness of Suffering." He continues by saying, *"The Bible also has a sober and realistic perspective on suffering. It affirms its un-thinkableness, its tragedy, its staggering and oppressive weight. Nowhere does the Bible forbid tears or portray them as a sign of weakness. In fact, it recommends them when we are in the presence of sufferers; Bible readers are called to "mourn with those who mourn.*[9]

While the Bible is quite clear that in the world we shall have trials and tribulations, it is still never really easy to accept, no matter from which angle it comes. According to John 16:33, *"These things I have spoken unto you, that in me ye might have peace. In the world ye shall have tribulation: but be of good cheer; I have overcome the world."* (KJV)

The Bible is deeply sensitive to our trials and tribulations. And make no mistake, our God does care about our hurts and pains as it relates to our suffering, which sometimes includes needless suffering at the hands of someone else's bad judgment. It can often cause a knee-jerk reaction to take place in our lives as a result of how others may have treated or responded to us or the hurts so many people face.

Especially when acts of injustice happen without any real, plausible cause, and no one in man-made authority steps up to the plate to make it right. It can and most often does make a very bittersweet pill to swallow no matter what the caption on the bottle reads.

Nevertheless, the Bible does have place within the confines of its pages where we can go openly to find some sense of solace and refuge. If we are but willing to enter in with our eyes open, the willingness to read and

---

[9] (Ortlund)

our ears willing to receive from the Word of God what it has to say, we find peace.

Pain is pain no matter if it is the loss of a spouse or a child. Pain can and will happen at the dying of a marriage you or I didn't want to or expect to let go of. Pain often challenges us when the sudden shock of losing our incomes or the loss of material things that meant sentimental value to us are without warning taken abruptly from us.

Pain is pain sometimes at the deepest level. It is in those moments in our lives when everything that earthly matters to us suddenly becomes so surreal—ready or not. And when our earthly world comes crashing down around us, ripped from beneath us, we look for solace and answers quite frankly from any place we can find relief. Hopefully that is through the Word of God. Sadly, however, some will choose another path or another method.

That brings me to how we as a people must learn to place our trust in God amidst our suffering, because He is the only true option we have. When I refer to "trusting" God, I don't mean by simply mouthing the words from our lips and our heads but not from our hearts with the utmost confidence.

When we look in the Bible, we find many stories as it relates to suffering. However, the one I want us to focus on right now is the story of the prophet Habakkuk who lived through a particular period of great suffering among God's people.

Habakkuk, like many of us today, when such tragedy and hardship comes our way, the first words or questions out of our mouth is: "Why me? How much longer is this going to last? What did I do wrong to deserve this trial in the first place?" Like Habakkuk, even when we ask God those questions, it is no guarantee His response will be the "exact" response we care to hear or receive.

Habakkuk lived in the time leading up to the exile of Jeremiah who lamented over the kingdom of Judah. He cried out to God about the "injustice and evil" he personally witnessed, which is ironically like our world today. Yet surprisingly, the response he received back then was not the answer he hoped. Therefore, it caused Habakkuk even more distress and perhaps confusion.

"For, lo, I raise up the Chaldeans, that bitter and hasty nation, which shall march through the breadth of the land, to possess the dwelling places that are not theirs." Habakkuk 1:6 (KJV)

As we can clearly see, God declared He was in fact rising up the Chaldeans—a brutal and terrifying people—to execute judgment on Judah for their injustice and transgressions. In other words, Habakkuk then had to struggle with how God could use that oppressive and wicked nation to deal with the problems among God's people.

It didn't stop there. Habakkuk cried out to God again, asking how God could use one evil to check another. "Why are you silent while the wicked swallow up those more righteous than themselves?"

According to Gary Ortlund, I believe God's response to Habakkuk then is what He is saying in response to our cries now, in a way. Because no matter how many times Habakkuk asked of God, God's response the second time was declaring He would bring or allow evil as a justification in the settlement of the overall score of wrong.

As we keep reading that scripture we find God does indeed have a plan. And His plan will be decreed and declared at its appointed time—no sooner or later than expected.

> *For, lo, I raise up the Chaldeans, [that] bitter and hasty nation, which shall march through the breadth of the land, to possess the dwelling places [that are] not theirs. They [are] terrible and dreadful: their judgment and their dignity shall proceed of themselves. Their horses also are swifter than the leopards, and are fiercer than the evening wolves: and their horsemen shall spread themselves, and their horsemen shall come from far; they shall fly as the eagle [that] hasteth to eat. They shall come all for violence: their faces shall sup up [as] the east wind, and they shall gather the captivity as the sand. And they shall scoff at the kings, and the princes shall be a scorn unto them: they shall deride every stronghold; for they shall heap dust, and take it.*

Habakkuk 1:6-10 (KJV)

It is important to note that in the end, Habakkuk did receive his answer, because he saw a vision of God coming in judgement and salvation to accomplish what He said would take place. The concern is do we always believe what

The Choice to Move Forward

God has said will actually be followed through with?

The other concern is will we allow ourselves to get into a state of "expectancy" from God? Which means on my end, I should follow up my request made unto God with serious intentions of doing whatever is necessary and needful to make sure I don't miss the move of God over and in my life. When God chooses to move in my life is up to God. My role in it all is choosing to "rest" and not sleep while God is working on my behalf.

When we get in the Word of God and learn for ourselves, He provides answers for us. Whether we fully grasp its full meaning at the moment or not, we know we can call on or ask the leading of the Holy Spirit to assist us in getting clarity and understanding by choosing to rest in God if nothing more. And we know because of God's track record over the keeping of His Word, we will be alright.

It is vital to know that asking a series of questions and even crying out to God is not forbidden. In fact it is welcomed. *"If any of you lacks wisdom, you should ask God, who gives **generously** to all without finding fault, and it will be given to you."* James 1:5 (NIV) God wants to be a part of every facet of our daily lives—the good, the bad and the ugly. He is big enough to handle any questions we bring Him, and He is trustworthy enough to see us through them as well.

It is important to note God may not respond or answer our questions in the manner we think or wish he would. But we can be assured He will do so in His own way and timing. What we can be assured of is He will come through for in His "perfect" timing for our individual lives.

Chapter 10 – Struggling With Suffering Is Real

> *"Glorifying God does not mean obeying him only because you have to. It means to obey him because you want to — because you are attracted to him, because you delight in him. "Jesus lost all his glory so that we could be clothed in it.*
> *He was shut out so we could get access. He was bound, nailed, so that we could be free. He was cast out so we could approach. This is what C. S. Lewis grasped and explained so well in his chapter on praising. We need beauty."*
>
> Timothy Keller[10]

The actual day of my beloved father's funeral and burial, the pain for me became so surreal. The inevitable earthly separation leading up to the actual day of his burial was becoming more and more unbearable as it approached. What I would have given to have another 24 hours with him, listening to his sense of humor,

---

[10] (Keller, 2013)

laughing and hearing him talk about God in such a personal intimate manner.

I hurt for myself as well as for my family—particularly, my mother, Frances. She was his beloved wife for over 50 years. Indeed, each one of the siblings was dealing with the hurt individually and in our own way as best we could. One thing for sure about my family I know for sure—when one hurts, we all hurt. Collectively, we genuinely care about each other's wellbeing.

As the day continued and we gathered at the repast, a dear sweet friend of my father approached me as I assisted in serving the crowd. I knew if I just kept myself preoccupied, I would not have to allow my mind to settle on the fact my dad was never going to grace this planet again. I knew the only way I was going to ever physically see him again would be in heaven.

I wasn't ready to let him go yet. I desperately wanted to feel his presence and hear his soothing voice at least one more time. So, as I served food and drinks, making nice with everyone, this woman appeared in my path. I am sure she really meant well. However, her words did very little to ease my aching pain when she said, *"Dear, keep your hands in the Master's hand, this will pass soon."*

I remember looking at her directly, refusing to speak at the moment, but choosing rather to simply smile. Inside, I thought to myself, *"Lady, this is not a puppy we're speaking about, this is my father. The man who raised me and took care of me. This is my father whom I will never, ever see, speak to, or laugh with ever again on this earth. Today, we had his funeral and now he is buried back to the earth. Ashes to ashes, dust to dust and all that remains before us is his incredible spirit* and the life he once lived being like a curtain blowing in the wind before all that knew and loved him. I wasn't interested in it passing quickly. I missed him now!

To me, and I am sure as well as for my family, all we had left were memories, joy and sadness and very real and raw pain. Plain and simple. All we had left were moments of silence sometimes and tears during others. We had a wife who found herself suddenly qualified as a "widow" who just buried the better half of herself. Yes, she still had her children. But how do you care for someone who, at least in her mind, was now grieving for herself the one person she had loved passionately for over 50 years? Knowing he is not coming back any time soon.

Honestly, quite frankly, I had no words, and I wasn't going to try to manufacture any in a matter of minutes. It wasn't the time. It wasn't the place. And it also wasn't necessary. I am the type of person, I don't believe "fake until you make" or pretend for the crowd. If I am hurting, I hurt. If I am sad, I am sad. But I must, in the moment, be my true self. And for those who can't comprehend that instance, keep living and I promise you the days are coming where you will not be disappointed.

In that very moment, we were all struggling just to remain sane at best. In that moment, no one sibling could afford to analyze the other's pain or judge the other on who loved and missed him most. In our own personal space, I am sure we would all received that award.

Of course some displayed their love more openly than others and in different methods and means. But our beloved dad was loved by each son and daughter. We all understood that being separated from your loved one is such a traumatic and sometimes dramatic event. Such moments after the death, funeral and burial at first glance can be very overwhelming and cumbersome.

Even though in "time" most of the pain will semi-subside, but it's not an overnight sensation that happens automatically at all. For me, it took much prayer, a whole lot of tears, reminiscing and thankfulness while remembering the good times we shared as a family unit. I realized, however, for others the suffering and separation of losing someone close to them comes in many, many forms and dynamics.

In that moment, what I learned and now know, is I didn't have the right, authority, power or the ability to condemn anyone else for how they grieved, how long they grieved or if they showed outward appearances of grieving. No one made me or anyone else experts on another person's emotions and feelings. After all, we all grieved and had the right to grieve in our own special way.

The death of losing a special loved one is never pain displayed as something simple to grieve. It is never about time, because in their world, they re-live the fact the individual they once held so dear is never, ever coming back again. No matter how much they grieve, cry or hurt—or in some instances get angry.

That moment in time is complete, at least on this side of the world for them. For those individuals, their suffering is real. It is tangible. And it is life changing for evermore. Especially if they feel they didn't get to say a proper goodbye. Or there wasn't enough closure between the two of them. Then of course you have the I wish I could of, should of, would of and the list goes on and on.

In fact, it is said that one of the deepest and most distressing treatments of suffering in the Bible can be attributed to the story of Job. By all intense and purposes, I would agree that Job was considered an innocent man who suffered much in a very, very short span of time. To me, his lost was unmeasurable and his pain probably unbearable. And for a while, he endured it all by himself without the help and or aid of "friends."

In those moments, Job's life was recorded as having lost "everything" he once possessed. And as if that wasn't enough, he suffered with terrible boils all over his body, which added more pain and suffering already to an unexplained amount of agony, defeat and open aggravated shame—people whispering, lying, pointing fingers and passing their open judgement.

Just like our world today, some people are quick to put their two cents in when one is undergoing various trials and sufferings. They never take time out for truth and compassion for others until it's their trial and pain. And like Job, here comes what Job thought were three of his friends who just happened to come for a, you guessed it, *"a visit."* Each one came with his own special gifts of accusations and guilty sentencing as an appetizer in tow.

Based upon what Job's *"friends"* had privately discussed behind Job's back concerning their own view points, they had concluded together Job must have done something wrong to cause "all this" destruction in his life. Once again, he that has no sin cast the first stone. Or in some cases, how about the first bushel of rocks.

Their reasoning for this was, "Surely Job must have provoked God in some way!" After all, to them, there was *"no other reasonable"* way! Job's friends had run out of all their man-made conclusions therefore, the only possible explanation for Job's sufferings were reasons caused by him alone. Sound familiar?

The bulk or most of the book of Job reflects on dialogues between Job and his friends in which they are admittedly trying to put the squeeze on Job to simply confess and come clean with his mistakes about how he got himself into this mess in the first place. They continued by saying, "Come on, Job, and confess! Tell us, what you did to deserve this?"

Pay attention to the special and kind phrases they used as his friends. "You deserved." "What did you do?" It's that way today, for some people. As soon as there is challenging or horrific news, sometimes those who you think know you best are the very ones who stand in an accusatory position against your character before they even know all the facts. In the words of my dear Mother, "But God!"

Thankfully, by the end of the book, God openly

reprimands Job's friends and commends Job. Afterwards, Job prays for his friends because he knew God was angry with them for how they had treated Job. Real talk, when I first read this story and in particularly this part, it took me about an entire month to handle it. I guess for me, the scene was just a little too real and raw.

The mere fact Job could actually have enough character, heart, integrity and godly desire to remotely want to pray for those who knew him best—and were the first ones to throw him up under the bus with the motor idling—gives him mega brownie points in my opinion. But need I digress.

I believe one of the many purposes of this story illustrated in the Bible is shown to us as a biblical reflection of suffering from a different concept. It is clear that Job, who had already lost "everything" in one of the most horrific manners speaking, could have literally lost it and just let his "so-called" friends have it right then and there. Instead, Job did not even attempt to defend himself but chose rather to allow God to fight the battle on his behalf. He chose to pray for his friends instead. This is p-o-w-e-r-f-u-l!

In other words, even though Job was hurting and in emotional, physical, and spiritual pain, he still had enough resolve left in him to bless his friends. He knew they could not possibly comprehend his suffering at that time. Job also knew the things he lost could not be compared to God who had provided them in the first place.

Most often, when trials and suffering attack us, the first point of reference we look to is the world's view for our understanding as well as direction in the moment. Very rarely does one, at the outset of suffering, look at the biblical viewpoint or principal prior to reacting about that situation. And by doing so, we cannot always comprehend why suffering happens in this life—especially to us or to those we love.

Like Job, for many of us, we may never understand the true purpose or cause of our suffering, no matter how many times we ask or beg God for answers. The point I am trying to make is suffering brings with it other hardships and insufficiencies. And even those very close to us can become overwhelmed just being in the shadows of what we are going through, let alone being able to endure it with us.

However, Job had to come to grips that logic, common sense or even thoughtfulness was not going to be a benefit to him in this moment. He needed an *encounter* with Almighty God himself.

No friends. No counselor to speak to. Just God on his own behalf. No banker, priest, pastor or life coach could do the job. Job needed to be fully *persuaded* that God was for him and pro him. No matter his hardship, even dire straits needs, the level of intensity his mega fold problems were, he had to come to grips and know his God alone was able. So Job had an *encounter* with God. We see that moment in Job's suffering (Job 38-41) when God introduces Himself to Job.

I find it is amazing when I am in a tight spot, and there appears to be no outlet near, God speaks to me in utter silence. No words, no comments, no smoking mirrors—just pure silence. No fanfare, no hoopla and no big announcements. Simply sheer silence.

You may say to me, "Then Brenda, how do you know if God is speaking to you at all?" My friend, that is a very valid and real question. You see, perhaps like Job, I am learning how to wait until my change comes. I am learning to yield faster than I ever could have imagined.

I am learning how to rest in the confidence of my Jehovah Jireh. I am learning how to come to Him with a serious praise and not a series of my complaints, problems, woes and mishap. I am learning how to bow before the King of Kings and Lord of Lords. I am learning how to give honor and adoration to the One and Only Redeemer of my soul.

I am learning how to acknowledge Him first in all of my knowingly ways and keeping my eyes and my hope upon the One who has been my sufficiency all of my life. I am learning to appreciate and validate that You alone, God, are amazing and a complete wonder to my soul. All of the godly Truth that Your Name alone is for my life.

However, I must admit while in the silence, that's when I feel the most calming sense of peace. Being still, not fretful, fitful, anxious or eager to move out of the shadow of His presence without His approval or covering. The silence no longer affects me like it used to, because I recognize God is in the midst of her (*Brenda*), right now. He alone will help her (*Brenda*) right early! Because Brenda chooses to trust, rely and rest in Him completely!

In that moment, no matter what the critics were possibly saying, his kin-folk were saying, the haters, doubters, even church-folk were saying, Job realized the choices he was about to make would depend upon what outcome he would receive for his pre-advanced troubles.

I believe Job must have taken a moment and thought about his perspective before choosing his words very carefully. Job had a flashback over his life and saw just how much God had already provided for him, and he didn't deserve any of it. Yet God had blessed him anyway.

Job understood not being happy in the moment of his trials and disappointments and yes, even in the midst of hurt, pain, loss and lack. Yet, he had a momentary *"wait a minute"* even while the reality of his pain was pushing him and plaguing him. I believe he still had a gnawing notion in his heart that kept on saying, "wait a minute."

You may be saying, "Wait a minute for what Brenda?" I believe the "wait a minute" was not only for Job, but we do well to have that "wait a minute" moment also. Job had to remember how good and worthy the name of God had been to him. Job had to realize God would never, ever leave him hanging in the balance.

Job had to come to terms that every setback means in the plan of God there is a supernatural setup for bigger, better and eventually greater! Job, like us, didn't fully understand his sudden situation. I mean one minute he had more than enough, and then within minutes and hours, he found himself in lack and degradation. Still, Job had a "wait a minute" appreciation.

Quick side bar to the readers of this book. I am challenging each of you to stop, breath, raise your hands up in victory, and say to the devil in hell, "I know you have worked hard and long. I know you must have employed your best bona fide demons and imps to take me out and destroy everything I have worked hard for and on. But Mr. Devil, what you didn't know was although you took the car, you took the house, you destroyed my marriage, you have alienated my children, you have separated my friends and you may even be working on my confidence. But Mr. Devil, as much as I hate you, I've got one more ace in the hold.

I've got a "wait a minute" in my spirit I've got to let loose on you right now. I am waiting before I declare defeat over my life. God is good all the time, and all the time, my God is good to me. I've got a wait a minute desire to reflect on one fact. God's grace is sufficient.

I've got a "wait a minute" spirit to thank Him for ALL He has already done and to reflect upon his goodness towards me and my family. I've got to thank Him for the things seen and unseen He has already provided for me. I must give Him praise and thanks for all the victories in and over my personal life, the deliverances I ain't told anybody about, and the grace and mercies I didn't even deserve."

I can just imagine that when Job saw God, he knew he no longer needed a response or an answer, because

Job knew God, Himself was the answer. How did Job respond? The Bible declares Job responded with joy and a repentant heart.

Praise the Name of the Lord! Like the character in C. S. Lewis's book, *Till We Have Faces*, Job concluded for himself, the discovery of when you come to know there is a certain kind of joy that comes from the True and Living God, that far supersedes anything we can think or imagine and even what we think we want.

Like Job, when we are going through our various trials and suffering what we really need most, more than our questions answered, is an ***encounter*** with God Himself. If we just get our questions answered, and not resolved to our satisfaction, they will only lead to more questions and frustrations later on. But when we are privileged to have a real "**encounter**" with the Master ourselves. Well, nothing else can compare.

.

Chapter 11 – The God Who Suffered On My Behalf

> *But he was wounded for our transgressions; he was bruised for our iniquities: the chastisement of our peace was upon him; and with his stripes we are healed.*
>
> Isaiah 53:5 (KJV)

When I think about this scripture, my heart literally yearns to get to know more about the man, the Savior, the King of kings, the Lord of Lords, the Healer, the Redeemer. My Everything who would pay such a priceless, unselfish debt for me that I will never be able to repay on my own.

I strain to get to know more about this God who chose to release and send His only precious Son on behalf of a girl who at the time didn't even exist in the womb of her mother yet. A girl who at this point had no real identity, name, purpose, cause or reasoning to exist. Yet this awesome God would permit her to be birthed in the earth at such a time and cause as this.

In fact, according to the scripture reading, from what I

have read this girl, me, would be known as an enemy at birth to the One and True Living God. She would be known as an enemy to the very one that ultimately paid such an incredible price for her life, so she would be set free one day through the blood of Jesus and His dying upon the Cross at Calvary. Through her acceptance of the Son Jesus Christ, she gets to reign with Him in paradise for all eternity.

Wow! What a Mighty God. In his book *Making Sense out of Suffering*, Peter Kreeft writes, "{God} didn't give us a placebo or a pill or good advice. He gave us himself. He came. He entered space and time and suffering."[11]

Okay. So I am a babe on a lot of things in Christ. But for the life of me, I cannot wrap my finite brain around someone who had and is All, leaving all Heaven had to offer to come down and willingly choose to pay such an unselfish cost. He spared no expense in paying the debt for me. I can't imagine His willingness to suffer and ultimately die such a heinous death for my sake and the sake of the entire universe.

Never the less, whether it's believable or not, He did just that for us. In the New Testament of the Bible, it teaches us Jesus was God in human form. We know through the readings of the Bible that He was born, He lived, and He died and rose again from the dead to defeat evil and to reconcile to God those who place their trust in Him. Now as simple and un-complex as those words may sound, the moments were far from anything serene. In fact, they were horrifying to say the least.

When Jesus decided to hang on that cross, He willingly

---

[11] (Kreeft, 1986)

chose to suffer the worst death imaginable. In addition, He chose to take on the sins of all humanity. This wasn't just a little finger prick. This was a horrible, traumatic agonizing death of the world. It didn't matter that He was innocent and knew no sins. He died for our transgressions anyway. It's all there, described in great detail—Jesus' death, burial and resurrection for everyone to read and accept.

What's interesting about the Bible is that it is not just some ordinary book, outdated with current information and events. It is not a book about advice filled with suggestions demonstrating the various methods of pain, suffering, and trials of this world. Fundamentally, the Bible is the story of how amazing and awesome our God really is.

It's a book about the incredibleness of our God. He is an all-powerful, all-knowing, all-seeing, and more than enough God. He is the God of wonder and might and amazement all rolled up into gigantic Majesty of greatness. He is the Alpha and the Omega of life. He is that hope and remnant Christians cling to for life—and that forevermore.

If we only could get a revelation about what God has accomplished for us and how He is repairing our broken world, our hearts and minds. That in itself would send a message of hope to us so we continue to believe and rest upon His name because of His love and kindness toward us.

The other day, I came across some interesting and powerful words written by a woman named Dorothy Sayers that I believe are noteworthy of repeating.

If Jesus was God among us, as the Bible claims, then we can no longer view suffering in the same way:

For whatever reason God chose to make people as they are—limited and suffering and subject to sorrows and death—he had the honesty and courage to take his own medicine. Whatever game he is playing with his creation, he has kept his own rules and played fair.

He can exact nothing from us that he has not exacted from himself. He has himself gone through the whole human experience, from the trivial irritations of family life and the cramping restrictions of hard work and lack of money to the worst horrors of pain and humiliation, defeat, despair, and death. When he was man, he played the man. He was born in poverty and died in disgrace and thought it all worthwhile.

Of course, the suffering of Christ does not immediately take away our own pain. In fact, Jesus assured his followers they would indeed have trouble in this life.[12] *But the suffering of Christ gives hope during tough times because it imparts something that is even stronger than suffering: the love of God, which the Apostle Paul called a "love that surpasses knowledge."*

As Tim Keller explains: If we again ask the question Dorothy continues, *"Why does God allow evil and suffering to continue?" and we look at the cross of Jesus, we still do not know what the answer is. However, now we know what the answer isn't. It can't be that he doesn't love us. It can't be that he is indifferent or detached from our condition. God takes our misery and suffering so seriously that he was willing to take it on himself."*[12]

The more I try to take in what my restricted brain can comprehend about the sufferings of Jesus on my personal behalf, it causes me to praise Him for His willingness to die for me and to pay the ultimate price for my soul and sinful nature. For that, I am eternally humbled, grateful and

---

[12] (Ortlund)

thankful for His goodness towards me.

Though our suffering is never easy, if allowed, through the Word of God, it does give us hope that one day our suffering will come to an end forever. And through the revelation of God's Word, we can cheat by reading to see we are given a glorious and magnificent vision of a coming world. One, which will demonstrate for all believers the end of all pain and suffering—gone forever. (Revelation 21:4)

One of the promising hopes is our God will wipe every tear from His people's eyes. The second hope is there will be no more death. Thank you Jesus. Or mourning, crying, or pain. For the old order of things will have passed away. I cannot utter what those words alone mean to me and for me. I do not possess the vocabulary to say so. All I do know is that I am very thankful.

The mere thought of God wiping away tears from the eyes of His people communicates not merely the close of earthly suffering, but consolation for earthly suffering. In the Bible, Heaven represents the place where sadness not merely ends, but becomes untrue—forever.

As C. S. Lewis wrote in his book *The Great Divorce*, *"They say of some temporal suffering, 'No future bliss can make up for it' not knowing that Heaven, once attained, will work backwards and turn even that agony into a glory."*[13]

There is no denying. The Bible offers this amazing

---

[13] (Clark, 1946)

gift of salvation to anyone who will believe in the Son, Jesus Christ, as his or her Lord and Savior. It represents the full and final payment of all of mankind's sins to anyone who repents of sin and trusts in Christ for salvation. According to the Bible, those who reject this salvation and persist in rebellion against God will be banished from God's presence and experience eternal death and suffering.

C. S. Lewis continues. *"According to the Bible, God already gave us the first installment of this beautiful ending when he resurrected Jesus from the dead. One day, what happened to Jesus—the reversal of death and liberation from decay—will happen throughout creation; the world will be redeemed and made new."*

The antidote will spread throughout the whole system. This vision of joy as the ultimate destination of redeemed creation explains our longing for permanent happiness and the feeling of being out of place we sometimes have in this world.

Likewise, Theologian G. K. Chesterton said, "Man is more himself; man is more manlike, when joy is the fundamental thing in him, and grief the superficial. Melancholy should be an innocent interlude, a tender and fugitive frame of mind; praise should be the permanent pulsation of the soul. Pessimism is at best an emotional half-holiday; joy is the uproarious labour by which all things live. Whether or not you believe in this vision of the triumph of joy and the undoing of suffering, you have to admit it is a beautiful thought."[14]

Overall, how we choose to respond to suffering is a path

---

[14] (Chesterton, 1908)

we all must choose within ourselves. For some, suffering brings out the worst in them and in their personalities. For others, suffering may cause them to retreat and withdraw from the world. Sadly, still for others, suffering can drive them to end their lives because to them, life holds no more hope, meaning or purpose for them or their lives.

Suffering oftentimes will produce very different results in different peoples' lives, depending on how they respond to it and react to its aftermath. For example, the same painful experience can make one person bitter, narrow minded, angry and even hateful and ungenerous. Yet it makes another person sweeter, humbler, and more patient because of the revelation he or she realized and received as a result of the situation. What makes the difference? Choices an individual makes to take away from the situation and the lessons learned in the moment. It can especially be difficult for someone who has experienced tragedy without an intimate relationship with God the Father. Often times that individual only looks up when he or she is in raw pain without a spiritual antidote to help ease the private pain.

One important aspect of the Bible's teaching is the call to persevere with integrity through suffering. In fact, it admonishes us to endure suffering like a good solider. *"Join me in suffering, like a good soldier of Christ Jesus. A soldier **refrains** from entangling himself in civilian affairs, in order to please the one who enlisted him."* 2 Timothy 2:3-4 (BSB)

In other words, the solider allows focus and energy

to remain on the matters at hand. He realizes he cannot afford to be double-mined at all during the battle or concentrate on the casualties. He must finish the job or assignments ascribed to him while still in the battle. Soldiers must not allow themselves to become ensnared with matters that are absolutely meaningless while the war is still raging.

The Apostle James taught that trials should be considered "pure joy" because they produce perseverance and strength that wouldn't ordinarily be utilized. The Apostle Paul took the concept even further, saying "suffering produces perseverance; perseverance, character; and character, hope."

The New Testament repeatedly calls Christians to stand up under unjust suffering, and even to rejoice in it in light of God's redemptive purposes. If allowed, suffering can sweeten and deepen us.

Or, if we choose, we can allow suffering to poison and embitter us and bury us in a bondage of isolation. Nevertheless, with God's help and our decision to endure and go on *through it*, we have a vital role in the end. We have a choice and now have experienced a conversation worthy of sharing with the world that perhaps have yet to discover our God is indeed able to bring us through.

Victor Frankl was a Jewish psychologist who spent years in a Nazi concentration camp during the Holocaust. Upon his release, he wrote about his experiences and observations. In his book *Man's Search for Meaning*, he wrote: "Everything can be taken from a man but one thing: the last of the human freedoms—to choose one's attitude in any given set of

The Choice to Move Forward

circumstances, to choose one's own way."[15]

I have learned in my latter years. No matter the suffering, trials, circumstance or situation. Whether it hits us so badly in the pit of our stomachs or knocks us to our knees. Whether we lose every earthly, tangible man-made sentimental value we ever owned. God's grace is so much greater.

I also discovered grace is not just a noun, but grace has a name and its name is Jesus. At His Name, everything else pales in comparison. I have also learned God's great grace meets us in places where we don't even realize gaping entrances were exposed to the enemy. While we could not afford to close them, the grace of God could—and did.

The grace of God is able to shield, keep, mold and protect us when we ourselves cannot find the strength, will or motive to even try to move forward. Sometimes life can hit so incredibly hard, it appears it knocked the very breath from our lungs. But somehow and some way, grace just keeps on abounding more and more.

God's grace is so rich it can make our insurmountable problems look like a simple molehill. It can cause stress to look like a temporary situation. Grace can take a problem and turn it into praise when we understand whose we are and in whose hands we have been placed.

As a final note on this subject matter—for those who are reading this book and still have questions about

---

[15] (Frankl, 1959, 1962, 1984, 1992, 2006)

the purpose and place pain and suffering have in our lives—take a look at this quote below. I think it says a lot and sheds some truth on the subject matter as it relates to suffering and theodicy.

Perhaps the most influential response to the Problem of Evil is the *"free-will theodicy" of Augustine of Hippo (354–430). Augustine taught that evil is simply the privation of good; it exists as a necessary possibility in a world of free, morally conscious creatures. According to this way of thinking, if God wanted a world without any possibility of pain, he would have had to create a world without any possibility of free choice or true love—a world of robots, not people.*

Another early strand of Christian thought, represented by theologians such as Origen of Alexandria (184/185–253/254), can be called *"greater goods theodicy." In this defense, God is said to permit evil because he is ultimately using evil to bring about greater good. Most people can identify with this at least to an extent; the majority of us can think of a time when something we thought was bad ultimately turned out to be good. If God can work out some evil for good, the argument goes, then isn't it possible—given enough time and wisdom—that he could work out all evil for good?*

Below is an additional testimony of a very noted journalist I thought were worth noting.

The Christian journalist Malcolm Muggeridge reflected on suffering in his life in this way. "Contrary to what might be expected, I look back on experiences that at that time seemed especially desolating and painful. I now look back upon them with particular satisfaction. Indeed, I can say with complete truthfulness that everything I have learned in my seventy-five years in this world, everything that has truly enhanced and enlightened my existence has been through affliction and not through happiness whether pursued or attained."

Chapter 12 – Looking Ahead Through a Different Perspective

In a desert land, he found him, in a barren and howling waste. He shielded him and cared for him; he guarded him as the apple of his eye, like an eagle that stirs up its nest and hovers over its young, that spreads its wings to catch them and carries them aloft.

Deuteronomy 32:10, 11 (NIV)

When we are in the midst of our pain and suffering, we cannot remotely fathom something good coming out of our situation. While persevering through, unfortunately for some, all we see is struggle, lack and insufficiencies. My dad would occasionally say something like, "Can't see the forest for the trees." Sadly enough I have quoted these same lines a few times myself.

However, there is no denying the world at large has met some courageous and special men, women, and children who have allowed their personal pains and tragedies to drive them to their greater good that will forever change the impact upon our world at large. Likewise, we can see some other examples of how our pain and suffering can be turned around for some common good as well:

Here are some examples taken from a website called "Why Pain and Suffering."

1. Pain and suffering can bring about creativity, resourcefulness and courage.

Example: Parents who lost a child helping to pass laws or starting organizations to protect other children. Artists and composers sometimes do their greatest work during times of pain or loss.

Scripture: Psalms 18; 42; 63; 126

2. Pain and suffering can help us to comfort others who are going through similar pain.

Example: This is the benefit of support groups for various problems. People who have faced the same problems are able to help and encourage others. John and Phyllis Clayton have been able to help others because of their experience with diabetes and with a mentally retarded child. Jim McDoniel has been able to help others because of his experience with a handicapped child.

Scripture: 2 Corinthians 1:3-5

3. Pain and suffering can help to shape our character.

Example: People who have survived as prisoners of war or persecutions often have a strength of character, which is admired by others. Gold is refined by the fire which heats it until the impurities come out.

Scripture: Isaiah 48:10; Zechariah 13:8,9; James 1:2-4

4. Pain and suffering can test us to show what we are made of.

Example: The patriarch Abraham was tested; Job, the ancient man of wealth was tested; the apostle Peter was tested; and the early Christians were tested. In all cases the testing showed the weaknesses and the strengths of their faith in God. Products which are sold in the marketplace are put through tests to find their weaknesses and to demonstrate their strengths.

Scripture: Genesis 22:1-14 describes the test of Abraham. The entire book of Job tells about Job's test. Matthew 26:69-75 tells about a test where Peter failed and he learned something about himself. Acts 4:1-21 tells about a test in which Peter was victorious and his enemies could see the strength of his faith. The testing of the early Christians is described in various places such as *Foxe's Book of Martyrs*. In Matthew 7:24-27 Jesus beautifully illustrated the results of testing in a simple story.

5. Pain and suffering can lead to repentance and salvation.

Sometimes it takes pain and suffering to turn a person's life around and head it in the right direction.

Example: The Israelites who repented in times of persecution in the Old Testament; Saul, who became Paul in the New Testament of the Bible.

Scripture: Judges 2:11-19 describes the cycle which the Israelites went through as they forsook their God only to be brought back to Him by suffering, and then to forsake Him again when times were good. In contrast to that Acts 9:1-16 tells the suffering which lead Saul the persecutor to become Paul the apostle, faithful to his God until his dying breath.

6. Pain and suffering can sometimes help us to trust God.

Perhaps we are forced to turn to God because we have no other place to turn.

Example: There are numerous people who have made the decision to trust God because of their pain and suffering.

Scripture: Job 40:3-5; Job 42:2, 3; Lamentations 3:19-24; Daniel 3:16-18; Habakkuk 3:17-19

7. Bearing pain and suffering well can be an inspiration to others.

Example: Chet McDoniel was born with no hands, only one stub of an arm and no thighs, but he has been an inspiration to many as described in the book *All He Needs for Heaven*.

Scripture: The apostle Paul endured his "thorn in the flesh" but was able to take the message of Christ to many areas of the world and write most of the New Testament.

We have to believe that the perfect will of God is not to harm us or to inflict upon us all malice of evil through pain and suffering just because He can. On the contrary, the will of God for our lives is polar opposite as it says in 3 John 1:2. *"Beloved, I wish above all things that thou mayest prosper and be in health, even as thy soul prospereth."*

(KJV)

We must choose to believe that whatever God allows into our paths will be and is for the common purpose of our greater good even when we cause some of those things through our own actions or knee-jerk reactions. Even when we have caused the sufferings and the misgivings through our own recognizance and disobedience, our God will still see us through.

There is never, ever a time when we will find God turning His back on us. Even though we may think so, or if the situation seems like He is not there, we cannot go by our emotions and our feelings, we must know by our trust and obedience in His ability to see us through no matter what.

We must learn how to speak life, wholeness, peace, and the truth of God over our daily lives and things that matter most to us. We must be persuaded that no matter what it looks like on the outside, we must choose to believe our God will always remain in our spiritual corner. He alone is more than able to fight EVERY battle if we are willing to stand still in His truth of it all.

Being still doesn't mean we get to play while being still; or simply go and sit down without a care, concern or focus at all. It means that we are being active in our faith and belief, choosing to trust and rest in God concerning the decisions, choices and plans that God has for us while we see the victory come through.

8. Pain and suffering can have a Divine purpose in preparing us for glory.

Example: The apostle Paul wrote that our suffering is

"slight" and "momentary" compared with "eternal glory."

Scripture: 2 Corinthians 4:16-18

9. Pain and suffering can prevent us from becoming dangerously proud.

Example: Again Paul said that his "thorn in the flesh" was to keep him from becoming proud and arrogant.

Scripture: 2 Corinthians 12:7-10

10. Sometimes pain and suffering in the life of one person can result in the advancement of the gospel in the life of another person.

Example: I know a family who accepted Christ because of the suffering of one member who died of cancer. The apostle Paul said that his imprisonment helped to advance the gospel.

Scripture: Philippians 1:12-14

12. Pain and suffering can allow us to be like Jesus.

Example: We are allowed to share in Christ's suffering as we serve the one who suffered on our behalf.

Scripture: Philippians 3:8-11; Hebrews 2:9-11; 4:15; I Peter 4:12-16[16]

---

[16] (Clayton, 2007-2015)

Section IV: Keeping Your Eyes on the Important Prize

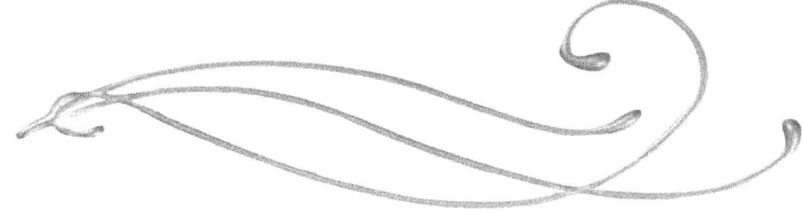

Chapter 13 – Don't Cast Away Your Confidence in God

Trust in the LORD with all your heart, and lean not on your own understanding. In all your ways acknowledge him, and he will direct your paths.

Proverbs 3:5-6 (NKJV)

It is difficult at best to keep your head up when the important things in life that really matter most to you and you alone seem to be moving at a snail's crawl or slipping away quickly and you still feel as though you have no resolve at all.

Even though you pray, believe, fast, trust and hope things will change any day now—even then, it seems like little to no progress is forthcoming. At least not at the speed you desire. In that moment, it is imperative to keep hoping more than focusing on the problem.

You try not to complain, at least out loud. You put on your best smile, square your shoulders and walk out in faith that today is going to be different. I can feel or sense it in the atmosphere. However, very little physically or emotionally—at least with the natural eye—has differed.

You know enough Bible scriptures and passages to plaster an entire wall. Yet, nothing in the natural is changing or has remotely changed. You are a born again believer and have been told you are the head and not the tail. You are the lender and not the borrower. Yet you cannot seem for the life of yourself to get ahead.

You have seen God do some amazing wonders in your life. However, the struggle is different this time, and it lingers despite your effort to believe, trust, obey and even pray. There are some days when you have more tears in your eyes than praise on your lips, even when you know our God is a good God. Still the proverbial mountain has not yielded, and you find yourself once again asking, "Lord, how much longer?"

I have found, for the most part, the problem can often be what we are saying and what we are demonstrating through our actions about our situations. Especially over our lives and our situations. What we are hoping for must become a greater focus and determination than what we are complaining and whining about in the moment.

The hope and the belief must both line up in our heads and our hearts until what we are truly hoping for begins to materialize in the spiritual realm and manifest itself in the natural realm. How long do we wait and hope? Well, I say until that hope becomes our reality.

"And hope maketh not ashamed; because the love of God is shed abroad in our hearts by the Holy Ghost which is given unto us." Romans 5:5 (KJV)

Hope is not meant to be this gigantic burst of energy that only lasts for the first 15 days of the month and then fizzles out by the 31st day of the month because outward conditions have not changed, or seemingly they have not turned around to our favor. We must learn how to "hope" until the end. Why? Because according to a blog written by Pastor Bill Randles our hope in our God is paramount.

"This is our hope, and our confident expectation. We don't 'wish for this', nor is this just a high ideal. The Christian has a hope, 'the hope of Glory', that is grounded in the very faithfulness and veracity of God. He that raised up Jesus from the dead will also quicken our mortal bodies.

That is why we can even rejoice in the midst of the tribulations we encounter here in the meantime. No longer do trials and tragedies and setbacks make us instinctively feel we are being punished by God, as they once did. The guilt has been answered for, therefore the fear is gone."[17]

We must continue to feed our spiritual minds with the Word of God and make sure what we are hoping for is aligned with His purpose for our life. We are challenged to hope until the end. The end of what? Until what we are hoping for has lined up with the will of God for our lives.

According to Hebrews 6:10-12, this call is a call to maturity in Christ not just a mere whimsical expectation from our lips to God to make us happy at a moment's

---

[17] (Randles, 2010)

notice or else. We've all seen how little babies and small children will literally fall out on the floor and become rigid, all because their parents did not or would not comply with their little wishes or demands.

They screamed out loud, crying as if someone is beating them or threatening their little precious lives. All for sake of building their little immature defense that their needs are truly immediate and must be attended right now on the spot. And when they are not met, watch out, because I am going to perform and act out instantly.

> *God is not unjust. He will not forget your work and the love you have shown for His name as you have ministered to the saints and continue to do so. We want each of you to show the same diligence to the very end, so that your hope may be fully assured. Then you will not be sluggish, but will imitate those who through faith and patience inherit what has been promised.*
>
> Hebrews 6:10-12 (BSB)

When we continuously make a decision to focus on God more so than on our problems and our temporary situations, the hope we have in Jesus Christ can and will stretch us in certain areas of our faith. It will cause us to literally surrender, throw our hands up and admit to ourselves, God I am nothing and can do absolutely nothing without you. I need you Lord!

Without that acknowledgment, we will inevitably give up and throw in the towel. We all have at some point in our lives secretly questioned God, became angry at God, and in some instances perhaps even doubted God. It looked like He just didn't care or at best was unconcerned about our trials and tribulations.

Still, even in those fleeting moments, you and I are challenged to be still and simply know He is God. But what does that statement really mean when you are at your deepest depth of despair and too overwhelmed to be still. That's like asking a three year old to sit down and conduct themselves like a well-behaved adult. Heck, some adults still have not mastered that term yet.

What do you truly say to someone who is at his or her wits end, and the days appear to be advancing? Days where loneliness, uncertainty, being alone, incomplete and solitude have become your newest best friend. How do you keep hope alive, fresh and vibrant in those trying moments?

Sure. You have a wonderful career, an incredible job or lifestyle or even your ministry appears to be at the greatest peak. Now more than it has ever been before or more than you could have imagined. But something still seems just a little off in your overall world.

Depending upon who you are sharing your heart with, some are quick to say, "Oh, what are you complaining about? There are others in this world who are worse off than you." Or "Let me tell you about my life. It's this, this, and this." Little do they know in that moment, it's not that you are heartless or anything, but in that particular moment, the only person or situation you care about is you. In that moment, you really need someone to listen and care about you.

Have you ever been in a place I call affectionately "there" and it doesn't matter how hard you work, how many Christian tapes you listen to, songs you sing, and prayers you pray. You can never totally escape that lonely place call "there" until and unless you own that specific moment in time in your life for what you are truly feeling. It feels as though you are about to suffocate from the sheer existence and weight of it all.

At the very least, the pressure just might stop you in your progressive tracks temporarily, because it seems too overwhelming for one person to handle. In trying to unload this insurmountable weight onto someone else, you may choose one you wouldn't normally trust to shoulder your load.

While having faith in God is vital, we must believe God will do what He has said He would do. However, trust is gas in the vehicle that transports us from merely believing to actually laying hold on what we have in faith, belief and hope. And still, I found I could do more to make sure the manifestation of what I am hoping for comes into fruition. That is having "confidence in God."

What does confidence means? Having confidence, according to Merriam Dictionary, means the full trust, belief in the powers, trustworthiness, or reliability of a person or thing: belief in oneself and one's powers or abilities; self-confidence; self-reliance; assurance: additionally, having confidence is also having the certitude; assurance: a secret that is confided or imparted trustfully.

Pondering the question of what does it mean to have confidence in God left me scrambling to do my spiritual homework, making sure I was in direct alignment to what I am really hoping I will receive from God. That led me to a specific scripture reference, Proverbs 3:5-6, which reads "Trust in the LORD with all your heart, and lean not unto your own understanding. In all thy ways acknowledge him, and he shall direct thy paths." (KJV)

There it was right before my very eyes in black and white. I was amazed at how straightforward the Word of God was regarding instructions for me to follow while I was hung up in that place called "there" and bordering on what's happening with my life as it relates to where do I go from here?

What I realized in studying this particular scripture was while I was focusing on the place called "there", I didn't realize I was trying to bring about answers and reasoning behind why I felt I had not received the particular things I was desiring from God by a certain timeframe. I was becoming frustrated in the process. After all, I was reading my Bible, praying my prayers and "*standing*" on the Word.

I felt like God was saying to me, "While all of those things are good, how about allowing Me to do the work and bring those desired things you ask into fruition at My appointed time and not your specific deadline?"

That was the missing piece for me. At His appointed time. I felt like the time asked plus the time I considered myself waiting and watching equaled enough time for Heaven's delivery.

I learned that day, although I am continuously in the school of learning. However, that day specifically, I realized having confidence in God meant to place my utmost dependency, rest, livelihood and obedience in the hands of an Almighty God that didn't owe me any explanation as to how, what and when He would bring me out or into my next season. Being given the privilege of expectation was a valuable gift indeed.

I needed to learn how to rest, rely and depend upon Him completely. Not until or when I thought it should happen. God was requiring of me, and is still requiring of me, to trust Him with my whole heart, mind and soul and not with my physical emotions alone. He wants me to solely rest and trust Him without any doubts He is with me all the way.

In that passage of Proverbs 3:5, having confidence in God means we must trust in the Lord with all our hearts, believing He is able and wise to do what is best for us according to His perfect will for our lives. Those who know themselves, find their own understandings a broken reed, which if they lean upon, will fail.

Most of us already know—depending upon what is being asked of us. In our humanness, to carry something without help and total dependency upon God, we have to understand , we would be unable, on many levels, to do so in our own strength.

So the mere fact we have God asking us to place our complete, unwavering trust in Him with ALL of our heart,

Keeping Your Eyes on the Important Prize

(nothing lacking, nothing wavering, everything on the line) choosing to believe He is not only able but is wise to do what is "best" for us is where the problem comes in. Many of us utter words that sound like we trust God. However, through our own actions, it is quite clear we are not really sure.

Now, let me be transparent for a moment. I don't have a problem with reading the scripture about trusting in God with all my heart. I don't have any problems about leaning on Him, especially when the pressures are burdening me. Where the nervousness for me tends to come into play is when the scripture says: "believing he is able and wise to do what is best." Now that is total control without my input at all. Wow!

I am thinking, "Lord the news about my health is not so great right now. I thought we had completely dealt with that two years ago, and I don't want to deal with that chapter again in my life." Or "Lord, the bills are due, and I really do not have the necessary funds to meet all of my financial obligations that I need for this month. What do I do now?"

God responds to me. *"Brenda, only believe." You see, it's not fast for 100 days, find 25 people to touch and agree or walk around the circumstances in silly circles until you think they are gone. No, it's a resounding, after you have prayed, confessed my promise over that particular situation or circumstance, thank me that it is already done. And now simply believe that I will and that I can, amen."*

And then you hear a response back. "...*believing he is*

able and wise to do what is best." And it puts you in timeout with the doubting and puts you back in the game of shifting your focus off you and back on Him where it belongs.

It also lets me know my trusting of Him should not be on whether He is going to deliver me in my way, but the outcome of either situation will be for His glory and goodness and my gratitude and appreciation for Him doing so.

Not only are we to acknowledge Him in all our ways, which proves sometimes to be quite uncomfortable on our end. We must also choose to believe our God has a hedge of protection around us, but we must acknowledge Him with submission. And when we do so, it is promised, He shall direct thy paths; so that thy way shall be safe and good, and happy at last.

Now, having said all of the above, according to Proverbs 3:5 Commentaries, I have to ask, are you sure you have confidence in God? And are you certain He is at work in your daily life to the point where you can let go of the earthly reigns?

Let's take the reliance test below:
Do you trust God in:
- providing for your needs
- forgiving you of your faults and short comings
- enabling you to overcome temptations
- giving you guidance
- restoring health to your body
- hearing and answering your prayers
- sustaining you through times of difficulty

- delivering you from the attacks of the devil
- and filling you with joy and peace[18]

My brothers and sisters, if you lack confidence that God is able and willing to demonstrate His power in every area of your life, then I have good news for you today. God, through his Son, Jesus is most certainly interested in us and wants to be intimately involved in our lives each day.

Just listen to the words of Jesus from the book of Revelation 3:20-21.

> *Behold, I stand at the door and knock. If anyone hears my voice and opens the door, I will come in to him, and will sup with him, and he with me. To him that overcometh will I grant to sit with me in my throne, even as I also overcame, and am set down with my Father in his throne.* (KJV)

From this scripture, it is very easy to see you can trust God with your past as you move forward into your promising future.

---

[18] (AlanP, 2011)

Chapter 14 – Trust God with Your Past as You Move Forward Into Your Promising Future

Trust in the Lord with all your heart; do not depend on your own understanding.

James 1:5 (KJV)

Every single human being has faith in something and anytime we demonstrate that faith through our actions, it simply means we are trusting, depending upon or relying on whatever we have "faith" in to do the job it was created or made to do. It is believing the chair we purchased from the furniture store will function in the exact same manner once we get it home.

Or, if the medications prescribed by the doctor will produce the results told to us at the visit to the doctor's office. Especially if the prescription is precisely followed, we think very strongly and/or believe every word told us.

Another sign of faith is when the brand new car purchased from the dealer last month will perform with the same precision and fine-tuning as it did when it was test driven with the car salesman and the auto dealer the week before with no sudden surprises. The bottom line is, we all have and demonstrate our faith in something or someone.

Faith in God is more than merely saying the words. To me, stating I have faith means a total reliance and dependency upon God for everything. God is reliable and you will never know that side of Him unless and until you relinquish everything to him. That means we cannot give him a portion and casually stash the rest of the goods away, thereby choosing to worry and fret about the rest as they are stored away somewhere in our private worry files.

Having faith means realizing God is not only bigger, but His Name alone supersedes, bigger, better and even greater than you and I—and being fully assured God wants the very best for us. He only has the very best in mind for us always. He wants to be the go to guy.

The first name I think of, not just in the bad times, but also in the good times as well is Jesus. He absolutely loves it when we cry out to Him for each and every one of our problems. He is the way out of no way. He is the answer. He is the Sovereign One, and He has the answer before we can invest the time to tell Him about our problems.

Having faith means "choosing" to believe God over every obstacle, over every trial and over every natural testing there is. Especially when storms clouds come and roost over our heads and they linger and hoover for hours, days, weeks, months and even possibly years. Choose to remain in faith even if the trial knocks you to your knees. At least we will be closer to God in prayer.

> *I have made up my mind Lord God no matter what comes into my life, my marriage, my finances, my career, my home, my ministry and my life, I need you God to be Lord over it all. I am nothing, I cannot do anything, and I cannot conclude anything without your presence in my everyday survival. Come Lord Jesus, and make your daily abode in my being. I am afraid to move without your hand upon my life.*
>
> Brenda Murphy

I choose to believe God loves me greatly. These last four years of my life have proven to me that you really don't know God in a particular area of your life until you get to know him in that particular area of your life. No one can teach you, forewarn you, instruct you, lead and or guide you into it. There must be sheer surrender and willingness that drives you there on your own free will.

It is a place, a journey you must take for your individual self. Just know that Grace goes before you and Mercy follows in hot pursuit behind you, making sure you will arrive on time according to God's scheduled. You will be securely covered on all fronts. In that place called "there," no weapon formed against you shall prevail.

Recently, I was listening to a statement made by Dr. Creflo Dollar that simply said, "Grace makes, and faith takes."

That statement almost knocked me to my knees in praise and worship. Knowing where I am in my spiritual walk with Christ today, I cannot afford to see it any other way.

I cannot go back in time, I must move forward in my faith and hope that God knows all and is in control over it all. However, I have never heard that Grace, who is a person, Jesus, makes all things possible for me to succeed.

I didn't know that through my belief and choosing to move forward to receive everything God has said I can causes me to take hold to the spiritual victory God has for me. Not just in the sweet by and by, but right now! Until that moment when I heard it for myself, I received fresh revelation I readily took hold of. Praise God!

The Book of Proverbs 14:12 says, *"There is a path before each person that seems right, but it ends in death."* (NLT) In other words, it is a dangerous thing to remotely put our hopes, faith, dreams, desires or even our livelihoods in the hands of anyone else, including ourselves, at any time.

While we are well educated and have plenty of life experiences, and we know somebody who may know somebody, there is no one like our God who already knows all. And He didn't just now find out. He is our Creator and Lord over it all. There is absolutely no one other than Jesus, and Him alone.

It is not that we cannot talk to others regarding things that matter to us. Yet, it is not a good thing to depend totally upon others to know what is best for us. When we do run to others for a place of refuge or strength, and we can no longer find it is a place of solitude or strength, not only are we majorly disappointed. But now, that place once thought a small piece of Heaven no longer holds that value for us.

That is the problem with relying on others for revelation all of the time or as the first point of reference. Our faith must extend beyond our human limited capacities. If we choose to go it alone without Jesus Christ, it is no doubt we will always end up heading in the wrong direction—even if it is with the best of our intentions.

Our human perception is not always reliable or necessarily trustworthy, because we are only capable of seeing our lives through inept lenses. In fact, the lenses of our vision and lives in and of itself are just good enough to make us *"think"* we're right – even when we're not.

Genuine and unpretentious faith is relying on God's direction and on who He is and what He is to you and me. It is sharing an intimacy with God for your own understanding. It is learning to rely upon God first and foremost before turning to others and trusting we have heard God correctly for ourselves.

God knows what you need, and He wants to meet those needs in His own timing and measure. Not only does God want to meet those needs, but He is the only one who is able and qualified to do so each and every time. In fact, He does not just meet them—He supersedes them without fail.

Keeping Your Eyes on the Important Prize

Unfortunately, for many people in the world today, we think we know better. We think we have a better plan. A better bird's eye view and a pulse on the overall problem, and we don't necessarily need God to step in just yet. So it is almost like saying to God, *"God, right now, I can handle things, but should they get worst or become over my head, I'll call you."*

We want to use our logic and our own judgment to get to the answer in a way that makes us look good and smart, yet doesn't require risk. But God wants us to grow. So He takes us a different way. A way that often has very little, if any, dependency upon ourselves, so He alone gets all the glory and honor due His name.

Many times in Scripture, God asks us to do what doesn't make sense to our logic. For example, Mark 10:43 say, *"Whoever wants to be a leader among you must be your servant."* (NLT)

To most people, that verse doesn't make sense. You'd think great people would have others serving them. Jesus says it's the other way around--the great people are the ones serving others. I need to trust what God says about greatness, not what I think.

God also says we're to honor Him by giving the first 10 percent of our income back to him. By our reason, that doesn't make much sense to us either. But we're to lean on God's understanding, not our own.

Because we trust Him, we obey what He says—even if it doesn't make sense to us.

For further study on this subject, consider this

resource. Tom Holladay is a teaching pastor at Saddleback Church and author of *The Relationship Principles of Jesus*. Saddleback Resources offers a small group Bible study related to these devotionals, *The Invisible War-Winning the Battle of Temptation*.

Chapter 15 – Decide There Will Be No More Wasted Energy

Our life span on this earth is always too short, even if you live to be one hundred years old. During our years, there are always lessons to be learned. One of the greatest lessons that I've learned is not to put too great a value on the things which can be easily replaced. But to cherish the irreplaceable, such as the people we love and time.

There is nothing more sorrowful than regret. Regret is like being on a ship that is slowly sinking without any signs of nearby rescue. It's the thinking over and over again of what ifs or why did I and never coming to a complete conclusion of the things we believe we could or should have done differently, if only we had another chance to do so.

After meditating, I personally realized that thought doesn't make sense. Even if I could turn back the hands of time, unless my "thinking" was diverted into the correct mindset, I would undoubtedly repeat the same cycle all over again. But for the grace of God.

The problem is who knows what the possibilities could have been? For some or even most, that second or another chance is no longer available at least in those exact instances.

Instead of agonizing over missed opportunities and lost chances, perhaps the best way to move forward is to learn from past mistakes and missed chances. And then make every conscious effort not to repeat the same mistakes again. However, the only way we do not is to seek God for wisdom.

I believe life has a way of sometimes repeating itself as it relates to do-overs. For example, say you were driving to work and someone was driving extremely fast behind you and rushing you through the light. When suddenly they decided you were going too slow and passed you up. They cut you off at an inopportune time and nearly caused your car to hit theirs as they pulled over immediately in front of you without ever tapping their brakes and then speeded off.

However, about a block or so further down the road, you find this same driver with their blinkers on because they have had an accident, and it is evident they could use yours or someone's help.

Of course you could simply pass them up and say under your breath, "Jerk. That's what they get for acting a fool." And keep going, allowing your conscious to get the best of you by choosing not to stop or slow down.

Say you made it to your destination, and for the rest of the day, you felt horrible. Although the other driver was totally wrong and rude, you realized you didn't have to respond in like kind. So you repent ask God to forgive you and say you will never do it again.

However, on the way back home, you guessed it. The same or similar situation reared its ugly head again. What would you do? Redeem yourself by choosing a different response or allow the cycle to repeat itself? Some of you need not cast your vote. Your response has already been noted ahead of time.

Choosing to re-live the horrible experience from this morning and justifying it by saying, "Why should I have to go out of my way to help them? I don't even know them. What I am trying to say, is in some cases, I believe God will allow us opportunities to have do-overs if we are sincere about taking the opportunity to correct a wrong when we didn't make a good choice about earlier. The problem is, we must be open and sensitive when those moments actually happen and make a decision to take full advantage of them.

"Christ loved the church and gave himself up for her to make her holy, cleansing her by the washing with water through the word." Ephesians 5:25-26 (NIV)

The good news for us today is we do not have to live with any more guilt, shame, regret, resentment or anger. Our beloved Savior, Jesus Christ, has already paid it all in full. God never intended for us to continue to carry around dead, unnecessary, wasteful weight that does not and will not add one iota to our lives, as if it were a specific trophy we won for being the most wounded victim on the face of this earth.

He has paid it all, and there is no balance due on our behalf. The sooner we come into agreement with God that we understand and accept what that means, the more delivered and free we are to walk out what truly matters as it relates to the purpose for which we are here on planet earth.

I have heard, "Brenda, you just don't know how difficult it is to let go. It is not as simple as you think."

You are absolutely correct, I don't know. However, I do know our Savior has extended to all mankind the invitation to cast our cares upon Him, because He alone cares for us. Sometimes the problem may not be casting the cares. It's the wondering how soon the cares will be cared for and taken away from our viewing.

The question is why do we choose to hold on to all our burdens and keep them packed in a clover sack, transporting them around from one relationship to another? Or live one bad decision to another, when we can simply release them and let them go?

Still at times, we are all too willing to carry one situation to the other, one problem to the other. Why do we go to bed at night and sleep with our trials, worries, pains, circumstances and heartaches as if it makes for a great pillow beneath our heads?

And in the mornings, we are eager to get up, get dressed, start complaining and then give our same trials, troubles and heartaches a ride back and forth to our designated journeys. Then, we start the process all over again. It's interesting to me.

For some, it may appear as a payoff to reflect how someone may have treated them unfairly and unjustly without cause. Perhaps, you feel if you hold on to the memory and the hurt long enough, it will be a way of showing the other person. Maybe somehow you're paying back the other person for the wrong they caused you. However, that is not a good idea at all, and it is certainly not the way the Bible teaches us we should handle the situation.

For the Word of God declares we should not return evil for evil but overcome evil with good. That kind of response can only be done through our willingness and the love of Jesus Christ. There is no sense in trying to pretend we can do it any other way, because we cannot. Even if we tried in our own strength, it will not last for very long.

Once again, we must remember it is never going to be easy to move forward if we deliberately choose to remain stuck by rehashing and reliving the story, the hurt, the wound, and the situation over and over again. As long as we keep the situation on ice only to thaw, heat or refreeze repeatedly, we are stuck in a no-win situation and an undelivered cycle.

If only we would choose to allow God to remove our bitterness, hurts and disparities and allow God to heal us from the inside out. He can, and He wants to without any scar tissue reminding us of the aftermath. We can be free to get on with our lives beyond our wildest dreams and expectations.

According to Pastor Rick Warren, *"God's Word cleanses the dirt, cleans up my mind, and washes my body. It gets all the dirt, the junk, the grime, the grit, the shame, and the sin out of my life. "The Bible says in Ephesians 5:25-26: "Christ loved the church and gave himself up for her to make her holy, cleansing her by the washing with water through the word." (NIV)*

So therefore, we just need to decide not to allow any additional wasted time, tears, resources, energy or thought to be given to a situation, circumstance, or problem God has already footed the bill for. We simply need to receive and accept that we are no longer in bondage and beholden to the enemy. We do not have to continue to walk around in sackcloth and ashes as though we have not been forgiven and released.

Below are seven scripture references that can help you with your struggle of regret.

Philippians 3:13
"Brothers and sisters, I do not consider myself yet to have taken hold of it. But one thing I do: Forgetting what is behind and straining toward what is ahead."

1 John 1:9
"If we confess our sins, he is faithful and just and will forgive us our sins and purify us from all unrighteousness."

1 Peter 5:8
"Be alert and of sober mind. Your enemy the devil prowls around like a roaring lion looking for someone to devour."

Psalms 34:4-5
"I sought the LORD, and he answered me; he delivered me from all my fears. Those who look to him are radiant; their faces are never covered with shame."

2 Corinthians 7:10

"Godly sorrow brings repentance that leads to salvation and leaves no regret, but worldly sorrow brings death."

2 Timothy 4:7

"I have fought the good fight, I have finished the race, and I have kept the faith."

Proverbs 13:15

"Good understanding produces favor, But the way of the treacherous is hard."

(These verses are all take from the NIV Bible.)

Chapter 16 – It's Working for Your Good

And we know that all things work together for good to them that love God, to them who are the called according to his purpose.

Romans 8:28 (KJV)

Months after having my surgery and well into my recovery time, I sat in my office one night after getting home from work with the lights off winding down for the night. Not really reflecting on anything in particular, I sensed in my spirit the Holy Spirit speaking.

"Brenda, the reason you still exist is not because of the great treatment you received from your doctors or the nurses. It is not because of the scheduled medications you take or the various prayers being prayed for you. You exist because my purpose is running through your veins. And as long as my purpose is running through your veins and you are doing my will, you will remain."

Immediately, tears of joy began to roll down my face. I totally received it and understood the statement. Not only was I appreciative and humbled by the words, I was grateful to God that He delighted in my desire to please Him. Even while my body was in the intermediate stages of being healed, I had already made up my mind I would develop a yet praise.

Why? Because this particular sickness had not been my first opportunity to witness the great hand of God upon my life. He had healed me many, many, many times before. However, being able to witness another opportunity to hear Him speak a word of purpose into my life was exciting and very well received.

Wow! It really caught my attention, because it caused me to think about my life and its sole purpose for existence in the earth now! I remember for years even while working in various churches, and being the leader over multiple ministries at the same time. Even though I was successful at carrying out what I believed to be the will of God at that time for my life, over time, I began not to feel fulfilled in what I was doing. I really felt the leading from the Holy Spirit for something greater.

It wasn't that I didn't enjoy what I was doing or the ministries I was a part of. I knew that particular season for that chapter in my life was over for me in that role, and it was time for me to move forward after I had completed the current assignment.

At times, even when I thought that season was over, I was very apprehensive to move forward with what I believed God was leading me to do. Not because God could have been wrong, but rather; out of fear and what I knew was going to be human backlash in the aftermath of moving forward, I allowed my wanting not to let anyone down rule over me. I remained "there" instead.

So I stayed much longer than I should have. More importantly, much longer than God intended for my life in that particular role in the ministry where I was residing. What I didn't realize at the time was even though it wasn't, and still isn't, my intention to ever hurt, wound or mislead others in anything within my control or responsibility. Nevertheless, sometimes it happens.

So the difficulty for me happened when I allowed the overall reactions and comments from others to cloud and hinder my true judgment of moving forward in what I know God was saying to me. By doing so, it costed me greatly. That is a life lesson I will forever be grateful for, though it was extremely painful. I am still grateful nonetheless.

During the early years of my life, I always knew God had a special call upon my life. However, like many others, I had no earthly idea what a "call" meant, let alone where the instructions for me to follow were. I had never been interested in being on a platform just for the sake of being or appearing to be "taller" than others who sat on the floor in seats looking up.

While others perhaps weren't ready, or didn't necessarily want to accept their call, I was the polar opposite. I was running full speed ahead to receive mine, even if I didn't have or know all of the answers to the place of the call. I was honored I had found favor in the sight of God, and that He wanted to use and include me in the completion of His will and purpose to make a difference on the earth.

I have always admired good preaching and thoroughly loved the preached Word of God. I absorbed its true doctrine when it was preached within its true context. God's Word is really liberating when it's taught correctly and not man-induced or interpreted for the sake of getting a well-intended manmade point across for self-glorification purposes.

God's Word always builds others up and never tears down or belittles. It encourages and never bruises others whether that individual is a Christian or a sinner. God's Word always provides life and never pronounces a death sentence on the hopes and dreams of others at their expense.

God's Word causes one to grow, to build up and expand their horizons beyond their wildest dreams, as well as extend an open hand to others to encourage, coach and assist them along the way.

It is important to understand this is just one of the many, many ways and means God operates. It does not mean everyone will share the same enthusiasm or willingness to share that piece of the olive branch with others.

In fact, in some cases, the enemy will do everything within his power to make sure that branch is never offered to others who have not accepted Jesus Christ as Lord and Savior of their lives.

For many, many years, I could not understand what the scripture meant in Romans 8:28 when it said, "And we know that all things work together for good to them that love God, to them who are the called according to his purpose" (KJV).

Of course, I could read it, but I didn't have a solid godly understanding of what it really meant to me personally—especially when I was experiencing some difficulty and hardship in opposition from the enemy at the time—just because I loved His name.

I thought, "God, surely the testing and trials I am currently being faced with cannot be used for my good."

I could not understand how that even fit into the equation at all. I honestly could not see how being put to and through a test of this magnitude could actually drive anyone closer to God, rather than away from His presence—until I learned how to trust God more.

I read a message from one of my favorite Pastors, Adrian Rodgers, dated July 6, 2010, when he talked about of course all things not being "good." But the Bible says, "We know that all things work together for good to them that love God, to them who are the called according to his purpose."

(1) In the chemistry of the cross God takes things that, in and of them, is bad, and He puts them together, much as a chemist might take chemicals that, in and of themselves, may be deleterious and mixes them to make a medicine that brings healing.

Many of us have some salt with our meals. Table salt is made up of both sodium and chloride. By itself, sodium is a deadly poison, and so is chloride. Put them together, and you have table salt. Salt flavors food, and a certain amount of salt is necessary for health and life. We cannot live without some salt in our systems.

God can take things that are bad and put them in the crucible of His wisdom and love. He works all things together for good, and He gives us the glorious, wonderful promise that He will do so. We know that we have victory over sin and over Satan, but this verse in Romans teaches us that we also have victory over our circumstances. It says that all things work together for good."

Pastor Rodgers continued to bless me by pointing out five specific promises found in Romans 8:28 concerning God working together to help me rise above my circumstances.

Certainty

The first thing is the certainty of the promise. Notice how the verse begins: "We know." (1) This is not conjecture, this is not happenstance, this is not perhaps, this is not maybe; this is ironclad certainty. "We know that all things work together for good" (1)–it's not a hope, not a vague opinion. Sometimes it may look as if God's plan ebbs and flows, but in God's timing His plan will be high tide. We can be certain. We live by His promises.

Completeness

The second thing is the completeness of the promise: "We know that all things work together for good." (1) That's a big promise, but it's there, and it's absolutely certain. God is a teacher who, by our standards, seems strange. He gives the test first, and then He gives the lesson. We learn through affliction. Think about Joseph in the Bible.

Think of all the terrible things that happened to

Joseph. He was maligned by his brothers. He was thrown into a pit and sold as a slave; he was lied about and accused of rape. Then he languished in prison.

But Joseph, as he looked back, said something that is much like Romans 8:28. Talking to his brothers, Joseph said, "As for you, ye thought evil against me; but God meant it unto good, to bring to pass, as it is this day, to save much people alive." (2)

Cause

The third thing is the cause of the promise: "We know that all things work together for good." (1) But don't get the idea that things inherently, in and of themselves, automatically work for good. Greek scholars tell us that literally the verse says, "We know that God works all things together for good."

In his Letter to the Ephesians Paul clarifies this point: "In whom also we have obtained an inheritance, being predestinated according to the purpose of him who worketh all things after the counsel of his own will."

(3) If there were not a God in glory, there would not be the promise of Romans 8:28 in the Bible. God is not dead. He is alive and well. He's not sick. He's not worn out. He's not even old. It is God who made this promise. He is the cause of it.

Condition

The fourth thing is the condition of the promise. It's not axiomatic, it's not automatic. The promise has a condition. What is the condition? "We know that all things work together for good to them that love God."(1) If you don't love God, you can't claim this promise. The condition is that we must be lovers of God. Haters of God cannot claim this promise. Some people may be able to sing better than we can sing.

Others may be able to teach better than we can teach, preach better than we can preach, lead better than we can lead, give more than we can give. But can we love God? That above all other things pleases and honors God. The first and great commandment is, "Thou shalt love the Lord thy God with all thy heart, and with all thy soul, and with all thy mind." (4)

Consequences

The fifth thing is the purpose of the promise. It is about those who are called according to His purpose. What is His purpose? In Romans 8:28-29 we read, "We know that all things work together for good to them that love God, to them who are the called according to his purpose.

For whom he did foreknow, he also did predestinate to be conformed to the image of his Son." (5) That's the key. What is the good that all things are working together for? To make us like Jesus. To be conformed to the image of His Son. There is no higher good than to be like the Lord Jesus Christ.

Many times this promise has been trivialized. For example, someone may be driving down the road and a tire will blow out. The person may say, "Oh, well, the Bible says that 'all things work together for good.' Maybe there's a sale on tires."

That isn't what this verse means.

The good is not to make us necessarily healthy or happy but to make us holy, to make us like Jesus. If the goal of our lives is not to be like Jesus, that goal is too small. Our goal must be to be conformed to the image of God's Son.

We may go through many dangers, toils and snares, but one day we will be like the Lord Jesus Christ. Whatever the circumstances that comes to us, we can rely on God's promise in Romans 8:28.

No matter our circumstances, no one can take this verse out of the Bible–and may Satan never take it out of your heart.[19]

---

[19] (Rogers, 2010)

Section V: Casting All of Our Cares Upon God

Chapter 17 – The Sweet Side of Victory!

Not only so, but we also glory in our sufferings, because we know that suffering produces perseverance, perseverance, character; and character, hope.

Romans 5:3-4 (KJV)

> "The greatest glory in living lies not in never falling, but in rising every time we fall."
>
> Nelson Mandela

What is your definition of victory? Is it winning at any odds? Is it always coming out on top no matter what the cost? Or is it being the one who stands out the most ahead of the crowd? According to Merriam-Webster Dictionary, victory is a noun that describes something that is completed successfully.

However, from a biblical standpoint, in the Old Testament when the word victory is used, the concept of victory signifies more than just a military conquest, though it includes that.

For many of the writers of the Old Testament, victory is ultimately something that comes from the Lord, and it is the Lord who carries on the fight, says *Baker's Evangelical Dictionary of Biblical Theology-Victory*.

The bible provides us with many examples of how victory was brought about. Throughout the bible we find examples of the Lord going with the Israelites in their conquest of Canaan.

He will fight against their enemies, and He will give them the victory. (Deut 20:4) Jonathan's role in Israel's victory over the Philistines was possible only because he and God fought together against the enemy. (1 Sam 14:45) David's defeat of Goliath was in fact the Lord's victory wrought for all Israel. (1 Sam 19:5)

David's conquest of the Edomites was a victory the Lord gave to David. (2 Samuel 8:6 2 Samuel 8:14) Similar victories, wrought by the Lord through human agency, are found in the stories of Eleazar, son of Dodo the Ahohite (2 Samuel 23:10 2 Samuel 23:12) and many others.

All ascription of victory must go to the Lord, for His is the greatness, power, glory, and majesty, as well as victory. (1 Chron 29:11) In fact, the prophet Jahaziel on one occasion communicates the word of the Lord to the people of Judah that they need not fight, but simply stand still and see the Lord's salvation. (2 Chron 20:17)

So complete is God's sovereignty in victory that He even gives victory to Syria through the agency of

Naaman, who is called a mighty man of valor, despite being a leper (cf. the angel of the Lord's similar words to Gideon in Judges 6:12).[20]

It is incredibly refreshing to know and fully understand our victory lays completely 100% in Jesus. It is not a separated thing. According to Exodus 14:14, *"The LORD will fight for you; you need only to be still."* The problem sometimes is when we want to be able to say we had some control and leverage in the reaching of our own victory in whatever the battle may be. Our first consensus should be that we take all of our burdens and care unto the Lord and leave (*meaning don't continuously worry, fret or allow ourselves to doubt*). Rather every time an opportunity comes for worrying, even if we can't do anything at the moment but lift up our hands towards heaven and utter, "Lord, I trust you in this situation," that's more than enough.

When we truly learn how to lean, trust, and rely upon the powers and the wisdom of the Almighty, All-Knowing God, we can sense our victory coming and it being a comfortable reach for us to receive by faith.

I am learning personally for myself that the things I am relying upon God for comes in several stages which are *pray, believe, rely, trust, faith, confidence and lastly expect.*

I have noticed when I talk to God through prayer and enter into dialogue with him in that order, and at times, I write down notes of my thoughts I want to express during my quite time in His presence. It serves as a tracking spiritual mechanism that allows me to be at rest. Anytime I want to

---

[20] (Elwell, 1996)

know what the progress is on my breakthrough, I can always refer to the status through one means or the other.

You may be wondering how I am able to do that and gauge what the true outcome may be? I don't know necessarily what the outcome is going to be. However, based upon His Word—because His Word is Him, and He alone is the Word—this is what I have found. James 1:6 says, *"But when you ask, you must believe and not doubt, because the one who doubts is like a wave of the sea, blown and tossed by the wind."*

Next, I layer my prayer with reliance upon God and not my own flesh. Back to Proverbs 3:5. *"Trust in the LORD with all your heart and lean not on your own understanding."* Then I make sure I am trusting in the Word of God by agreeing in advance with Hebrews 11:1. *"Now faith is the substance of things hoped for, the evidence of things not seen."* Then being 100% assured that He has heard me, I bring it on home with Philippians 4:13, which gives me the confidence that *"I can do all things through strengthens me" (NASB)*

The most difficult part I find sometimes in allowing God to fight the battle for me is in my willingness to relinquish and release *all* control to him without any input on my part for its outcome.

So many times when I have been wronged and it looks like the other party is having fun at my expense, it can be quite difficult to simply stand by and watch from afar. However, I now know that is exactly what the enemy wanted me to think was happening—that God was not moving on my behalf, not just in the correcting of the other person's mistreatment of me, but helping me through the difficulty I was facing as well.

Chapter 18 – No More Delays

> "For I the LORD will speak, and whatever word I speak will be performed. It will no longer be delayed, for in your days, O rebellious house, I will speak the word and perform it," declares the Lord GOD.
>
> Ezekiel 12:25 (NASB)

A few months back, I was invited to a church service with a really great friend at the last minute. I decided, based upon the church's theme for that night, "**No More Delays**," I had to attend, no doubt about it. Nothing prepared me in advance for this meeting. It was unusual and exhilarating all at the same time and very much worth all the hustle and bustle to get there.

The ride to the church service was very much anticipated by me and my friend as we chatted on the drive over there. We were both trying to speculate on the move of God for that night's service. After arriving at the church, we realized the service was already in progress, and the Spirit of the Lord was definitely already set in motion.

We were ushered up to the front of the service where there wasn't the slightest possibility of missing a thing. I was very, very excited to say the least and so was my friend, Sister C I call her. Although she had attended services there on many occasions prior to this particular event, as I observed the service, I noticed the men and women on the program to speak that night generated a posture about the service that stated, "God is in the building. Expect a move of God at any moment during the service." Boy oh boy, was I ever stoked!

As the service continued throughout the night, each speaker's message began to build upon the other's following consecutively behind the other as if they were in a tag-team match. However, there was something special about the eighth speaker's posture. It appeared to be saying, I am here for business only. I am primed, I am pumped and I am prayed up to get the victory! I am telling you this gentleman really stood out the most to me.

He was a tall, dark gentleman, beautiful smile, determined personality and a robust posture. He was focused during the entire service. When the speakers before him spoke, he appeared to be very in tune and engaged. However, I could immediately tell by his demeanor that he came for business in the will of God, and he wasn't leaving the presence of God until manifestation was completed.

The moment his feet touched the floor and he was introduced to the audience, the Spirit of the Lord within him was unleased without restrictions. You could just tell. It was remarkable to witness and meaningful to behold.

He spoke very rapidly in tone and with a very heavy

African dialect, yet he spoke without a hint of nervousness, doubt or hesitation. It was as if he was reading off of a television prompter. His voice was strong, deliberate and persuasive all at the same time.

He didn't mince words as he moved about the sanctuary in an engaging manner, being determined and concise to connect with his audience and demanding our attention from the moment he stood before us.

While I was being mesmerized by the presence of the Lord through him, at the same time, I could also sense the presence of the Lord being radiated from his person, confidence in his direct relationship of God being in his life.

There is something about an individual who really has a divine connection with God. It is not something that can easily be "acted" out. It shows through our mannerisms—in how we walk, talk and carry ourselves in and out of public view.

This gentleman displayed such presence before the audience. I remembered the speaker reading several scriptures as he continued to minister. However, there was one specific scripture reference that resonated within my soul, and that was Ezekiel 12:25.

> *"For I the LORD will speak, and whatever word I speak will be performed. It will no longer be **delayed**, for in your days, O rebellious house, I will speak the word and perform it," declares the Lord GOD.* (NASB)

As a young girl, the book of Ezekiel was one of my most favorite books of the Bible. Often, I would read it at least several times a month and cry at the exact same point of reference, *"Can these dry bones live again?"* Even as a young kid, I always thought and believed that these specific words had a lot to do with the outcome of my personal journey, and I was correct in thinking so.

As the night continued with this speaker, he kept referencing the phrase, *"No more delay! No more delay."* By the third time, he turned around and challenged his audience to say it with him over and over again until it was coming from our hearts and not our lips.

One of the times he was saying *"No more delay,"* he said, *"If you want something from God you must be willing to do whatever it takes, even if it means not looking cute in the process."*

I was sitting there thinking to myself, "Wait a minute here, this gentleman is on to something." He is not just chanting some words, but he is being very, very specific about a particular need and purpose. So I leaned in more determined to receive from God that night whatever his true intent for me was. I knew deep in my soul I wanted more of God, and I was not leaving until I believed I had received from Him my heart's desire.

Because he was moving and quoting scriptures upon scriptures, I was unable to keep up. However, I was able to write the book and chapters down for later review. Choosing instead, I paid closer attention, as to not overlook anything important that was happening right before my very eyes. I didn't want to miss anything God was doing that night in that room.

After he finished ministering, he declared and decreed specific scriptures over our health, in particularly, "cancer," "tumors" and "pain." Each time he mentioned those three specific attacks, he became more and more determined and intentional. Tirelessly, he continued to pursue the Blood of Jesus over the congregation.

Even while doing so, he challenged us to cry out to God for ourselves. At some point, he stated that when we pray, we should expect something on our behalf from the Lord, and we should also declare them in the Name of Jesus to take place.

He was careful to tell us that not only was he and the other ministers going to continue to pray for us, we were encouraged to do the same and after each declaration he would say, "No more delay!" And so would the audience.

Without a doubt, the room that night was permeated with the praise, power and potency of God the Father. There was absolutely no denying that truth at all. For the most part, everyone in the room appeared to be connected and plugged in to the bigger force present that night, and we were all on one divine accord.

In the end, he called for everyone to please stand to their feet, and he said, "I am going to pray for each of you." He invited other ministers to the alter to join him in praying and believing God for those of us who were in the household of faith that night as well.

After placing my offering into the basket, I approached the minister and asked him to pray for me. Without the least bit of hesitation, he proceeded to do so with fervency from the power of God from on high.

While I was not necessarily trying to resist the presence or power of God in the room that night, I couldn't help but to take notice as the minister laid hands on me, the electrical immediate effect I felt running through my body once his hands connected to the top of my head. The divine connection of his hand being placed on my head felt like 100 volts of electricity coursed through my entire body in a matter of seconds it seemed.

In that moment, there was complete surrender from me unto the power of the Holy Spirit and sheer rejoicing in the presence of God without struggle or hesitation. He continued to cry out to God on my behalf as I lay out on the floor in complete yielding unto the Lord by faith. "Lord, no more delays, and no more delays," I heard him say over me time and time again.

In the days following that particular meeting, I could not get the passage of scripture out of my mind. Over and over again, I just kept thinking about No More Delay! Finally, I looked up the scripture reference for myself, and there I found specific things that spoke to me about what I had been privately praying to God for answers.

"For I the LORD will speak, and whatever word I speak will be performed. It will no longer be delayed, for in your days, O rebellious house, I will speak the word and perform it,' declares the Lord GOD." Ezekiel 12:25 (NASB)

What a Word! I love the fact that the scripture very boldly states, *"For I the LORD will speak, and whatever word I speak will be performed. It will no longer be delayed."* To say I was blessed at the reading of this particular passage of scripture would be an understatement. His Word didn't say, I will try to make it happen. I'll see if it can happen, but a definite I will speak. Whatever word I speak will be performed. And it will no longer be delayed.

No one but God can be that bold. Deliberate. Assured and intentional. Now, the most important part about this declaration hinges on His Name and His Word only. It is not predicated or conditional upon man coming into agreement with God, or for that matter, even believing whether or not He can and will do it. For out of the mouth of God, He has spoken it and therefore, it is so.

After the service that night, as we drove home, I was ecstatic about the good news. In my heart, I had already laid claim to my healing, financial situation and my breakthroughs.

I wasn't going to wait until I could see the manifestations, I believed God and moved out on faith that it had already happened for my good that night. So I began rejoicing in advance and expecting great things to take place in my life from that point on.

More than ever, it had become apparent to me I needed to start rejoicing and believing God more and focusing less on my problems and situations. I was beginning to understand and embrace the fact that while declaring and decreeing is vital for my life, stepping out in faith was going to be the priceless key that had to become my number one priority.

I knew beyond a shadow of a doubt that without faith it was impossible for me to remotely please God. As a child of the King, in order for me to receive anything from God, I knew I had to learn how to lay everything I am and hoped to be on the alter and leave it there before God. God loves to be trusted—especially when we cannot see anything positive before us.

In the days ahead, I just kept reciting that scripture and saying out loud, No More Delays. Each time I proclaimed the Word of God over my life, I felt my spirit connecting with my confidence in God, that He was in agreement with my heart felt request.

So often, the enemy of our time wants us to be fearful of his intentions in our lives, and he wants us to live in fear of what we think he can do to us. The more we focus on those possibilities, the more leverage he will gain over our thoughts and eventually our decisions.

That's why I am a firm believer in advocating that we should be filling our minds and thoughts with the unadulterated Word of God several times throughout the day. For me, it's got to be the Name of Jesus in the morning and Jesus throughout the day, because the pressures and stresses of this world are designed to steal our joy and rob us of our peace in Christ Jesus.

As the people of God get more into the Word of God and study for ourselves, pressing in to know God more and

Casting All of Our Cares Upon God

more and relinquishing our limited understanding for His wisdom and guidance, we will began to see massive changes in our overall well-being. Our God loves us, and He wants to bless us and be involved with every decision we make—in fact, before we make them.

The enemy of this world is forceful and intrusive in our thought lives. He wants nothing more than to destroy us by aiding us in our negative thought behaviors through doubting God's Word for our lives and encouraging us to move ahead of the plan of God for our lives.

He will whisper in our ears at our lowest times about how much God doesn't love or care about us. If we don't have enough Word down in our spirit to combat that lie, He will win the victory over us in the moment.

And when that happens, we have become victims of another one of the enemy's scams of lies and deception. Once our belief of faith has been hacked into by the greatest liar himself, Satan, it can at times be difficult to trace where the faulty spam mail came from.

All we know now is that we have willingly accepted the false information delivered to us through false pretense. Now the virus of the enemy's lies has begun to spread through our minds, emotions and thought life, leaving us to deal with a very arid and depleted outcome of defeats, deterrents and trajectory about our situations.

There is only one way to stay ahead of the enemy and beat him at his game. We must make sure our passwords are up to date, changed frequently and placed in a secure place where no one or nothing unauthorized and without the proper identification code can enter in.

We must change our password from victim to victorious. From defeat to deliverer and from hopelessness to hope in God, because we are no longer looking within ourselves to take care of us. But rather, we are consistently looking to Jesus, the Author and the Finisher of our souls, to be our complete source and resource.

No more delays to me means we must discontinue our old ways of thinking through our daily living and performance and start making the Word of God a priority each and every moment of the day. We cannot afford to treat God like He is a special guest, visiting with us only on Sundays. It isn't enough to simply invite Him into what should ordinarily already belong to Him.

God should not be just a welcomed spectator on the wall waiting to see if we need Him, but rather understanding we cannot enter into the throne room of praise and worship until the King has been honored and received in our hearts first. He should not be looked upon as being the "featured" guest but the Owner, Keeper, Redeemer and the Finished work of our entire being.

Until the day we acknowledge Him to be Lord over all, we are only kidding ourselves and living underneath our means. Not just material means but rather our entire means. Everything we are and hope to be is in the hands and the will of God for our lives. Someone might say, well I work and earn my own way, God is not doing that for me, I am the one going to work every day.

While parts or that entire story may be true, you must not stop there. Continue by asking yourself this question. And by whose might and strength are you moving in? Who provided the opportunities and the abilities for you to do so? Who sustains you while you work, and who makes the provision for your vision to come about?

No more delays represents to me that those things God has purposed and planned for my life are going to come into fruition at its appointed time and order. In the meantime, my soul purpose should be to make God's Word my daily priority above any and everything. My desire should be to live my life in such a manner that God will always be first in all things concerning me.

Understanding that God alone is the source of my life should become the fuel and the motivation behind my praise. In fact, when I lay down at night and begin to count my daily blessings, I already know they are entirely too numerous to name or imagine. As I continue to align my ways with the ways and mannerisms of God's purpose for my life, I believe I will continue to be blessed in every manner.

Chapter 19 – Empowering Quotes for the Soul

> *"I believe that we are solely responsible for our choices, and we have to accept the consequences of every deed, word, and thought throughout our lifetime."*
>
> *Elisabeth Kubler-Ross*

> *"Life is a game and your mission, if you choose to accept it, is to play fully."*
>
> *Wendy Hearn*

"Nobody gets to live life backward. Look ahead, that is where your future lies."

Ann Landers

Life has no limitations, except the ones you make."

Les Brown

"Today is life - the only life you are sure of. Make the most of today. Get interested in something. Shake yourself awake. Develop a hobby. Let the winds of enthusiasm sweep through you. Live today with gusto."

Dale Carnegie

Chapter 20 – Overview

And He who searches our hearts knows the mind of the Spirit, because the Spirit intercedes for the saints according to the will of God. And we know that God works all things together for the good of those who love Him, who are called according to His purpose. For those God foreknew, He also predestined to be conformed to the image of His Son, so that He would be the firstborn among many brothers.

Romans 8:27-29 (BSB)

"You will find that it is necessary to let things go; simply for the reason that they are heavy. So let them go, let go of them. I tie no weights to my ankles."

C. JoyBell C.

We have covered a lot of ground thus far dealing with past hurts, rejections and pain from our lives. Each of us are at various intervals in our personal journeys. Some of us are

Casting All of Our Cares Upon God

just entering into that specific walk due to fear of what the emotions and raw feelings attached to our mental thinking might bring out. Sometimes, we would rather hold on to the heaviness of it all in an attempt to heal ourselves from the inside out without any help from outside forces.

I thought this quote from C. JoyBell C. was entirely too thought provoking to simply pass over. I agree very strongly with the writer in saying indeed there really does come a time in life when it is not only feasible to let some things go, but it is healthy to set them free from our spirit.

If we are determined to hang on to what cripples and reduces us to negativity, gossiping or unforgiveness and bitterness, we will never achieve the purpose of why we were placed on Earth in the first place. Sad but true, some individuals even armed with this knowledge would still rather choose negativity rather than being set free in Christ.

From time to time, I cannot tell you how much it saddens me to see a man or a woman troubled and plagued with mountains of guilt and condemnation of their own unforgiveness. Things they may have done in the past they have refused bitterly to let go and allow God to change in them for their good.

Sometimes, I see them walking down the streets with all their little earthly possessions on their backs and typically no place to go they can call their own. Literally bent over in their stride, but not because their personal belongings are too heavy. Quite the contrary. But because of unresolved issues they do not often desire to own up to.

You see, until I am willing to become humble enough to acknowledge the entire forest in my eyes, I really should not be able to see the couple of twigs in yours. One of the primary problems in the world today is not the economy nor who ends up as the next president of the United States. It is our own innate ability to feel as though we are the ones, and our needs that should be catered to, stroked, taken care of and should have "*first priority*" in all things.

The word of God clearly tells us to lay aside the weight and those things that can cripple our strides in the Lord. We ought to strive even more, especially in our day and time to let go of anything that does not bring hope, life, peace and wellbeing into our lives. Just decide to lay it aside and get ourselves into position so we can finish our races in a timely, godly, well-balanced fashion.

Weights bring about constraints, and constraints limit our ability to move forward and do so accurately and efficiently. In fact, in the King James Version of the bible, the definition for constrain is to bind, to strain; to exert force, physical or morally, either in urging to action or in restraining it; to confine by force; to restrain from escape or action; to repress.

No matter what we are up against in our lives, and no matter the difficult challenges and situations we find ourselves in, we must choose to believe our God will never leave us nor forsake us. He is always right there with us in the battle. And because He is at the head of the battleground, we will walk out with the victory if we are willing to maintain our peace and focus while being in the midst of our personal storms.

The mere fact that some of us have carried our trials and pains around—from relationships, strained commitments, jobs, careers, marriages and divorces, the death of a loved one or what-have-you—is not only unhealthy. But I believe our God is grieved by one mere fact. Here He is, reaching out to us with opened arms and a willingness not just to help us shoulder the load, but to actually relieve us from that burden in its entirety—at no further cost or determent to us. And our response sometimes to Him is *"No thanks, I've got this."*

> *"People have a hard time letting go of their suffering. Out of a fear of the unknown, they prefer suffering that is familiar."*
>
> Thich Nhat Hanh

Yet for some, if not most of us, we are determined to wear the scarring on our person, as if those scares are a representation of a badge of honor to the world. Look at me. I have gone through a horrific divorce. I was in a marriage of 30 years, and one day my spouse simply walked out. I was devastated and cannot bring myself to move on. Sweetheart, you better. He or she has.

Another example: Perhaps you are the one elected,

or so you think, in your family or among your friends or co-workers to be a blessing in general. However, you feel that no one ever feels the need to help or give back to you. Left unaddressed, you will become bitter, hateful, despondent, changed, hostile and downright resentful at the thought of those individual's lives moving forward.

In fact, all you can see through the lens of your eyes is "How can they be so blessed, when I have helped the entire world, and I have nothing to show for it at all." Can I tell you that is a very dangerous place to be, because the real anger is not with the person whom you feel defrauded you in some manner and left you holding the bag.

However, your true anger is with the Almighty God but you are too afraid to approach Him with your findings. So you continue to hold what you believe unfounded, unnecessary unforgiveness and borderline hate against your brothers and sisters whom you walk around seeing daily.

Oh you may say, "That's not me, I am not mad at anyone. I have a pure heart. I love everyone." You think? Are you sure? Well before you respond, you may want to look at the situation through the lenses of God instead of your old contacts or bifocals, because the prescription could be outdated.

You see if any part of that statement were true, you would not be able to recall everything about that person you just stated you have forgiven them for when anger rises up in you. You would not be so easily offended just by their mere appearance before you.

You would not become jealous at the mere fact they

were blessed sometimes through their labor and work ethics that God blessed them to do through His strength to get that house or car or great job.

All you can see is the fact that they currently have or possess the very thing now you deem you should have gotten and instead of them. After all, you deserve those things through your good deeds. Well, they are not good if you only did them for vainglory and self-righteousness. The Word of God clearly says when we show alms in public, we have already received our rewards.

I am so glad God really knows what's going on. And there are many upon many other examples out there in the world today. In fact, they are too many to try to list. We must be careful to examine ourselves in making sure we are not holding on to yesteryear's pain out of the sheer need to feel or to remain victimized in some way or in control of others destinies.

Let it go so you can grow effectively into the will of God for your life.

I don't deny that one's pain to them can be and is very real. However, what I am saying is that when there is a better way offered out of our pain so the healing processes can begin, so we can continue to grow in a godly manner, we should by all means take it and run with it. And never, ever look back.

In fact, we should be careful not to make a memorial or a place of worship in which we pay homage to the very pain and trepidation or the bad memories of the past, choosing to visit its gravesite through our prison of select memory once a year. Let it go for the betterment of the person we are aspiring to become.

We should allow our past hurts and abandonments to become our springboards for new development to our future rather than allow the hurts, pains, and various stigmas to become a headstone for our past. To become memorials by which we willingly choose to pay homage annually by revisiting them.

In all honesty, we look back and choose to remember and remain focused on some of our hurts, pains and disappointments. Many of these happened during a time in our lives when we made bad choices out of our ignorance or not understanding there was a better way of doing things. We should choose to be very busy thanking our Heavenly Father that He decided not to leave us in our mess.

When we remember those personal times without proper guidance in our lives or no real role model in whom we could base our choices against, we should be busy magnifying our God's name with a thunderous voice rather than stewing in anger and hatred.

When we realize how much of a mess we were in and could still remain in, but God! We should be on our knees with our hands lifted up in the air, giving our Father in Heaven the highest of our personal praise, instead of plotting and looking for underserved retaliation on another person.

I am telling you, we all have much to be thankful for and lots to be forgiven for, and ain't nobody more worthy of praise and thanksgiving but our God. No one can get the glory for coming out of our mess and our nasty attitudes and grudge holding selves but God.

Every time we think about holding malice and hatred in our hearts for one another, we should think about how much the blood of Jesus covered for us. Those thoughts should make us very quick to forgive and choose to move forward.

I fully understand some don't readily know how to move forward. You may or may not have ever experienced a personal relationship with the Lord. Maybe you are just getting to know the Lord personally, and before that time, you may have simply received bad advice over the years about forgiveness and followed too many wrong examples from others who were misled themselves.

The list and options are endless regarding unforgiveness. Nevertheless, none of those adjectives are a reason today to hang on to the unnecessary and useless pain we refuse to let go of each day.

God desires for us to be totally free in him, not bound and restricted, chained and shackled by old hurts and condemnations. It is not God's will for us to be held up in our own makeshift personalized prisons just because it affords us a look out through the bars every now and then.

We must wake up and know we have already been declared as the righteousness of God but not by our own doing, input, making or perfection. It was all given to us by the blood of an Almighty God, and nothing and no one else contributed anything!

> *"Some people believe holding on and hanging in there are signs of great strength. However, there are times when it takes much more strength to know when to let go and then do it."*
>
> Ann Landers

I strongly agree with this quote from Ann Landers. Sometimes, we tend to think, "If I just hang in there a little bit longer or look the other way just a little while longer, then maybe—just maybe—things will turn around in my favor. Or hopes the person will treat me differently, all the while knowing inside, the likelihood of things changing own their own is like trying to locate a needle in the haystack way out in the woods.

In fact, it's quite the opposite. If we are ready to get on board with God's desires for our lives and gain access to the greater things scripture refers to, we must become active in our own roles designed for our individual lives.

We must choose each and every day to read the Word of God for our own lives. But not just read a bunch of chapters and verses. We must take care to believe and practice what we have read on our own lives first before we challenge others to do the same. We cannot just sit around idly wishing and thinking someone else is going to swoop in and rescue us from our misery. "Forget the former things; do not dwell on the past." Isaiah 43:18 (NIV)

The Word of God is adamant about us forgetting the former things that hold us down and restrict us from moving forward with our lives and in the grace that was paid for by our Lord and Savior Jesus Christ back on Calvary countless years ago. Why? Because my suspicion is that He knows we cannot carry out the will of our Father looking back, being bogged down with entirely too much dead weight and regrets from the past.

So where do all these old feelings of regret, remorse, doubts, fears and resistance to change or the dwelling on past mistakes come from? Well, we need not look any further than from the originator of lies. Satan is the mastermind of bringing our past mistakes to the forefront of our thoughts. The sad thing is for some of us, we don't just hold on to our past. We delight in holding on to the past of others, which is none of our business.

Satan tends to remind us right before we are ready to take steps of faith how undeserving we are. How we should not hold out any hope of being blessed or moving forward. After all, according to him, look at how wretched and meaningless our lives are. Look at how many times we have messed up the will of God for our lives and embarrassed Him (as if he cares). He claims God could never forgive us for all of our past mistakes and sins.

Yet we must resist dwelling on our past mistakes

and continue to speak the Word of God to opposing thoughts. We must denounce Satan's attacks as soon as they speak to us. The devil and his demons can't stand the scriptures being used against their condemnations—they will flee. We must not just become content with speaking the Word of God, but we must be equally convinced and confident that those very words we speak have authority over the devil and all his demons.

"But one thing I do: Forgetting what is behind and straining toward what is ahead, I press on toward the goal to win the prize for which God has called me heavenward in Christ Jesus." Philippians 3:13-14 (NIV)

The Word of God encourages us to stop dwelling on our past and reach toward our calling instead so the kingdom of God can continue to be built up in Jesus' Name. Do you realize that the more we procrastinate in our decision to move forward in the call and will of God, someone else, somewhere else, will miss the mark or opportunity to know Jesus as their personal savior? You may say, "I don't think so. I am only responsible for my own walk and my getting to know Jesus."

1 Corinthians 10:31-33 reads, "So whether you eat or drink or whatever you do, do it all to the glory of God. Do not become a stumbling block, whether to Jews or Greeks or the church of God, just as I try to please everyone in all I do; For I am not seeking my own good, but the good of many, that they may be saved.." (BSB)

As Christians, we should take care not to use our liberty to hurt or offend others, or cause offense to their own reproach. We must strive to be that example in the world among many who are looking and longing for a relationship with God but don't know how to go about it.

Therefore, while we are determined to walk around in sackcloth and ashes because we refuse to let go of the past, no matter how difficult it was, the bigger picture states we must let go in order to affect the work of the kingdom.

Whether it is in our eating and drinking, and in all we do, we should aim at the glory of God first and foremost. Our number one daily goal should always be aimed at pleasing and honoring our heavenly Father even before attempting to please our needs and wants.

You see, when we make the purposes of God our highest priority, we will always have all our needs met. One of the most critical parts we consistently fail to realize is that we have not served God until we have served his people. And that's one another.

> *Then the King will say to those on His right, "Come, you who are blessed by my Father, inherit the kingdom prepared for you from the foundation of the world. For I was hungry and you gave Me something to eat, I was thirsty and you gave Me something to drink, I was a stranger and you took Me in, I was naked and you clothed Me, I was sick and you looked after Me, I was in prison and you visited Me."*
>
> Matthew 25:34-36 (BSB)

Above all things, we are called to renew our relationship with God from our past mistakes. Why? Because through the shedding of Jesus' blood at Calvary, He already paid the entire bill. Therefore, we have no godly right to continue trying to collect for a debt that has been fully paid for by someone else.

In others, I didn't and couldn't pay my own sin debt. Now what makes me think I have the right to collect on the debt of my natural and spiritual brothers and sisters? I have none!

At the shedding of Jesus blood, we were all set free to move about the earth in the Name of Jesus. We were all set free to make sure His perfect will is done through us, especially those of us who are Christians. No one came into this world with a different set of options. We were all born into sin and our lives were expressly shaped into iniquity—but our God!

"Create in me a pure heart, O God, and renew a steadfast spirit within me." Psalm 51:10 (NIV)

I believe the longer we refuse to let our past go and continue, determined to hold on to our past wounds, we are deliberately choosing to disobey God. Now, we are sinning—willfully choosing our fleshy influences to override the purpose of God's will for our lives. In other words, we willingly choose to walk around in hate, dislike, unresolved issues and meanness because our flesh doesn't want to let go for our own selfish reasons and motives.

Perhaps you may be one still saying, "But you just don't know what I had to endure over the years. How they treated me. How much I had to take."

And Jesus is saying, "You just don't know how much I had to pay at the cross, prior to the cross and even now while I am watching you daily choosing to willfully disobey me by holding on to stuff that no longer serves your purpose and my will for your life."

He says, "If you want to surrender your past to me, I will gladly handle it and take it from you. However, you must desire and ask Me, 'Create in me a pure heart, O God, and renew a steadfast spirit within me.' In other words, you may come to me but your heart must be in a position to want to be delivered and made whole and to move forward."

Why? Because God knows our sin always separates us from God. We can feel distant from Him just as Adam and Eve tried to hide when He approached them in the garden. However, God doesn't want us to run away from Him—He wants us to run toward Him. He is our Father in heaven who loves us with a great and everlasting love.

> *For if you possess these qualities in increasing measure; they will keep you from being ineffective and unproductive in your knowledge of our Lord Jesus Christ. But whoever does not have them is nearsighted and blind, forgetting that they have been cleansed from their past sins.*
>
> 2 Peter 1:8-9 (NIV)

We can choose not to remember our cleansing from

past mistakes by continuously dwelling on the negativity of our past. In some cases, we don't dwell on our past mistakes. But neither do we completely forget our cleansing from sin. A great and awful price was paid—namely the crucifixion and death of Jesus Christ—for our sins. We must strive toward living a purposeful life in the Lord instead of becoming like the world.

How do we do that? By choosing to reflect on God's goodness toward us in spite of our past mistakes. Psalms 25:7 encourages us, "Do not remember the sins of my youth and my rebellious ways; according to your love remember me, for you, Lord, are good." (NIV)

God is good to everyone on the earth—the believer and unbeliever alike. Yet when we come to know Christ, we are completely forgiven and cleansed by the blood of Jesus. We didn't deserve His goodness. Therefore, we need times to reflect and meditate on His love, grace, and mercy toward us. We need not sit around and waste our entire lives on regret and misfortunes of what happen to us years and years ago.

We can also get beyond the past mistakes by being filled with the Holy Spirit, which will compel each of us to move forward to completing the mission of His calling. Getting bogged down because of our past makes us ineffective and a hindrance in ministry. We cannot possibly point others to Christ when we ourselves still have not forgiven or moved forward in our own lives.

We must learn how to deal with the consequences of our past mistakes with grace and wisdom from the Lord. We cannot possibly correct things on our own and in our own might. It takes God's grace, mercy, wisdom and willingness to do so.

Without that mindset, we are doomed before we even begin. But we can do so with God's guidance and love dwelling on the inside of us. Then, and only then, can we honestly get pass the past mistakes!

> *"People have a hard time letting go of their suffering. Out of a fear of the unknown, they prefer suffering that is familiar."*
>
> Thich Nhat Hanh

About three years ago, I started attending a class on Wednesdays called affectionately, "Cop Talk." Over the past three years, this class has been a place of refuge and growth for me personally. I enjoy mainly the class interactions and the ability for our class to pray for one another before and even during the time spent together.

The topic of forgiveness comes up often, if not weekly. We discuss things like learning to let things go quickly. We understand the longer we leave old hurts and wounds unattended, it quite often further aids us in the refusal of letting go of what we may deem as bigger things, thereby causing us more damage than necessary. We realize our lives should be touched, not strangled. And when we refuse to forgive and let it go, we remain stagnate and torn.

> *"We must be willing to let go of the life we've planned, so as to have the life that is waiting for us."*
>
> Joseph Campbell

On the positive side of letting things go is the amount of space we free up to accept new possibilities God desires to bring into our lives. The new divine relationships He desires for us to connect with, the new opportunities He would like us to embark upon, or new challenges He has prepared for us to explore wait on our readiness. The enemy would like nothing more than for us to quit too soon. Or simply throw our hands up in the air and declare defeat.

As for me anyway, I cannot do that. I have fought through too many challenges. I have seen God do some amazing, incredible and miraculous things in my own personal life to quit now. I cannot lie and say I always know exactly how He is going to deliver me from the snare of the fouler. But what I know to do is keep my head up and declare I know He will come through as He has always done for my family and me in the past.

Today, I choose to believe He loves me, and believe His desire for my life in accordance with 3 John 1:2. "Beloved, I wish above all things that thou mayest prosper and be in health, even as thy soul prospereth." (KJV) At the end of the day, I choose to believe those are more than just mere words to my soul. They are God's truth.

> *"The mental and physical space we create by letting go of things that belong in our past gives us the option to fill the space with something new."*
>
> Susan Fay West

What an incredible powerful statement! The very idea of letting go of things that no longer serve us value and fill up room to grow is powerful in its own right. When I think about holding on to past wounds, hurtful situations and relationships that, quite frankly, did not serve me in the moment and definitely didn't contribute anything to my future, I get a little upset with myself for doing so.

Even when I know the difference between catering to and really, really letting go of some things I know are not better for me on all fronts, over time, I find myself coddling some of those thoughts as though they were vital to my future well-being.

I realized I am a visual person. So to help me move forward and leave old mentalities and mindsets behind, what I can imagine myself doing naturally actually helps me in the spiritual realm as well.

I decided to do some spring-cleaning in my entire

physical house literally during the summer. I didn't wait to see if I could no longer wear a certain outfit before I gave it away to someone who could probably use it now. Great idea. However, the thought of giving them away did not come as easily as I thought it would be. In fact, I found myself at times, moving the same items from stack to stack and from place to place within my house before making the decision finally to give some of them away.

I believe at least some of the reasons why I had such difficulty doing so was because the items chosen were personal. The thought of giving away things I once wore to a complete stranger somehow frightened me just a little. And then I began to question my decision, at least for a moment.

There were other items I gave away, like bedspreads and comforters, in hopes they could be used or given to someone who might not have the luxury of purchasing those items for themselves.

In the process of cleaning out my closet and "giving" away personal items that meant a lot to me at the time, I still found myself not wanting to depart with those items. Quite frankly, some still held a sense of sentimental value to me although I could not wear all of them and t had no further use for them.

I discovered that the more I gave away intentionally, the more free I felt on the inside. That space provided me the room literally to move around more in my home without being restricted. I thought maybe, just maybe, that is the way God wants me to be in my thinking about letting go of old doubts, heartaches, pains, wrongs, disappointments and let

Casting All of Our Cares Upon God

downs. Mentioning any of them, even today, saddens me.

> *"Lovely days don't come to you, you should walk to them."*
>
> Rumi

When I read this quote, I realized if I were to move on to brighter days in my heart, I was the one who needed to start the journey in daily expectation and not the other way around. I cannot expect change if no work within my own willingness to change is happening. I so desire lovely days ahead, and I want lovely people around me to share those moments.

> *"Start now. Start where you are. Start with fear. Start with pain. Start with doubt. Start with hands shaking. Start with voice trembling but start. Start and don't stop. Start where you are, with what you have. Just…start."*
>
> Ijeoma Umebinyuo

The number one reason this quote is so powerful to me is because I know all too well it is true—at least in my heart. We cannot be afraid to try something different or new just because we are unfamiliar with what the outcome or what the journey might be.

There is something extremely profound and liberating about starting where you are. Even when you are afraid, unsure of what lies ahead, shaking and trembling while in motion, decide to forge ahead still. While even in your speech you are unsure of your own words, try anyway. Move forward any way. Refuse to quit. Stop or turn around. Trust God to finish what He alone began in you, taking refuge in the fact He has already spoken through his word.

> *"The LORD will deliver them up before you, and you shall do to them according to all the commandments which I have commanded you. Be strong and courageous, do not be afraid or tremble at them, for the LORD your God is the one who goes with you. He will not fail you or forsake you." Then Moses called to Joshua and said to him in the sight of all Israel, 'Be strong and courageous, for you shall go with this people into the land which the LORD has sworn to their fathers to give them, and you shall give it to them as an inheritance.'"*

Deuteronomy 31:5-8 (NASB)

Whatever you do, decide to move forward and become a better you. In fact, don't just become a better person, be all God has created, ordained, called and equipped you to be. Once you start, make up your mind to finish strong, no matter who may not be able to go with you, who decides the cost is too high to go with you or even those who may not think you will even make it. Leaving absolutely nothing undone or unspoken, in the Name of Jesus, make up your mind to stick to the promise or the commitment at hand and finish what God alone started in you.

> *"In the end you can't always choose what to keep. You can only choose how you let it go."*
>
> Ally Condie

In the words of one of my good friends, "Our God is Almighty!"

I love hearing those words, because they are true and accurate. Our God is indeed Almighty. There is no mistaking who He is and that He in fact reigns over all and in all. He doesn't have to solicit the aid and assistance of anyone at any time concerning you. He is God alone!

If we only could see in the mind of God how much He loves us and desires only the very best for each of us, I am sure we would be blown away. Personally, I love to say this phrase, "One of the very best gifts that God ever gave mankind was the gift of choice." I truly believe He wants us to desire Him out of sheer free will, not force.

Ally Condie's quote, "In the end you can't always choose what to keep. You can only choose how you let it go," is a perfect scenario about the choices we make in our lives. Whether we intentionally choose good, bad or indifferently, the choices are still ours to consciously make. We can choose to remain deliberately stuck in old mindsets, attitudes, deeds, actions, reactions, gossip, lying, hating, scheming or being selfish and controlling. That is still the lifestyle we deliberately choose.

Therefore, when the consequences of what we have chosen return to us in a not so flattering manner, we must not deny the fact it is what we drew in because of our own behaviors and actions. But still remember, if any of those actions look and feel delightful to us, it's because we chose that behavior. It isn't a God's gift to you.

Section VI: The Final Decision Is Up To You

Chapter 21 – Final Words; Think on These Things

And the peace of God, which surpasses all understanding, will guard your hearts and your minds in Christ Jesus. Finally, brothers, whatever is true, whatever is honorable, whatever is right, whatever is pure, whatever is lovely, whatever is admirable — if anything is excellent or praiseworthy — think on these things. Whatever you have learned and received and heard from me, and seen in me, put these things into practice. And the God of peace will be with you.

Philippians 4:7-9 (BSB)

I can remember when I was first introduced to this passage of scripture, and I remembered thinking to myself wow! I wish it was that simple. It seemed no matter how hard I tried to think all day on positive things, the more my mind was being bombarded with other thoughts. I honestly didn't think I invited them in.

On my own, I tried relentlessly to "think on these positive things," but my mind, at times, attempted to more often than not, revert back to the days, times and events of yesteryear's old wounds and past hurts. With those thoughts came unwarranted and unforgiving thoughts of anguish sometimes.

What was painfully clear during those times, was the afterthought and emotions I was always left with. Feeling emotionally drained from remembering the exact moment when disbelief settled in. And when disappointments followed suit as though I had just experienced those initial hurts and old wounds for the very first time.

I remembered a sickened sensation of badgering myself with why didn't I respond differently in the moment. Why didn't I speak up and protest louder against the enemies torturing? Why didn't I call and end to the blatant games that were being played in the process of the lies being told? Believe it or not, most of the time, I was too concerned about hurting them and their feelings. There were moments, even feeling desegregated from the rest of the crowd, that I questioned myself as to why didn't I stand up for myself more in the wake of the bullying or the obvious under tone and snide remarks? Or at least immediately dismissed that person out of my life as opposed to continuously subjecting myself to undermining words and sometimes actions that did not support or encourage me for my good.

I didn't know that while no one can totally control their thoughts or keep them from happening; we don't necessarily have to succumb to what we are thinking about. If we are mindful of what we are thinking, we can rebuke those thoughts. Pull them down from having total dominion over our actions to those thoughts, or simply choose to dismiss the thoughts from becoming actions or reactions entirely.

It's funny now but not so funny in times past. I remember watching television late one night, and I didn't think I was hungry. Especially not for a "McDonald's Big Mac." Well—not until I saw the commercial on television. It seemed like within every couple of seconds, I saw that commercial over and over again, until it became a part of my psyche. And then all I could think about was that hot, juicy cheeseburger dripping grease from the bun.

I thought, "Well, McDonald's is just right around the corner. It won't take that long to go and come right back." Got you. I thought later as I was devouring that cheeseburger like nobody's business, what an easy target I was.

Now I realize, the more I focused on every little detail about that commercial, the more I was being reeled in like a fish on a string. All the subliminal messages and sound effects were in place just for that "particular" moment. Even the hues in the picture were designed to reel in people like myself in that moment, who were too busy focusing on thoughts and fleshly emotions.

Looking back at that moment, what I should have done was denounce the desire and craving of what I didn't need as opposed to continued watching of the screen. I allowed myself to become engulfed in the emotions of satisfying my taste buds.

I didn't grasp that the longer I allowed my eyes and emotions to play a major role in my decision making during that commercial, rather than listening to my heart and wisdom screaming, telling me no. Just look away, or better

The Final Decision is Up to You

yet, turn away from the temptation altogether—and turn off the television too boot. I willingly gave myself permission to be drawn into this unnecessary web of deceit.

Of course, afterwards, the guilt, condemnation and embarrassment was all I had left to contend with. I didn't stand in truth that I really didn't need the hamburger, it was unhealthy for me to eat it at that time of night, nor was it necessary for me to go and get it, because I was not even hungry at that time.

I was angry with myself afterward, because I knew I had the ability and power within my control to make better choices and decisions in the moment. Through the inability to look away and even walk away, even though I felt myself being reeled in, I inevitably surrendered my truth for the lesser. Instead, I allowed myself emotionally to be drawn in as if I had no choice.

This is exactly what this scripture is trying to say, perhaps in a more profound example than mine. Nevertheless, you and I can get the gist of what I am trying to demonstrate.

The writer of this chapter wanted us to pay closer attention to our thought life and the patterns and things we meditate and repeat over and over again until it forms a formidable vicious life cycle. Filled with regrettable bad choices and influences, which leave us wounded and oftentimes bewildered.

> *And the peace of God, which surpasses all understanding, will guard your hearts and your minds in Christ Jesus. Finally, brothers, whatever is true, whatever is honorable, whatever is right, whatever is*

pure, whatever is lovely, whatever is admirable — if anything is excellent or praiseworthy — think on these things. Whatever you have learned and received and heard from me, and seen in me, put these things into practice. And the God of peace will be with you.

Philippians 4:7-9 (BSB)

Finally, we can see that our reward will be in our favor when we trust our emotions, our will and ourselves to the Almighty God. He is more than able to lead, guide, direct and steer us in the right direction each and every time in everything. Our God never fails.

The Word of God tells us very boldly, not only should we think on the positive things, the things that build us up. The things that bring godly joy, motivation, peace and genuine happiness into our lives is exactly what we should be thinking about. When we allow ourselves to be filled with the Word of God, we will realize what we have learned and received, we can now put into practice. The things the Word of God desires to put into us allows us to experience and become engulfed with the peace of God—to know where we are today is exactly where we should be in Christ.

Now on my way to the greater things He has for me up ahead.

This verse couldn't be any more correct. I can tell the difference when I am meditating on things that are honorable, joyful and valuable, versus when I allow my mind to travel back in time on things that were hurtful, demeaning, unproductive and on and on they go. When those thoughts take place, I feel the very fiber of my emotions rise up to the occasion as well. Even just thinking about a negative moment in my life brings with it the emotion attached to it. I cannot really do it just in trying to explain all the particulars, but I do know for sure it carries with it all the aftermath of that thought.

It really doesn't matter if the betrayal, hurt, sadness, disappointment, the loss, devastation or insult happened weeks, months or years ago. The mind is so very powerful. It can bring about such tremendous emotions, trauma and feelings until you think it took place a few seconds ago and is still very much raw in your being.

Likewise, when we experience wonderful, spectacular and joyful news to celebrate, we feel as though we have something tremendous and incredible to celebrate. Our hope goes through the roof of life. Our faith is on high alert, and not even the enemy himself can steal, borrow or rent our joy.

On the other hand, when we take our eyes off the Word of God and allow ourselves to turn our minds and attention inward, we often focus on who we are and what we think we are able to do within our own might. We began to sink in our own disparity, not fully coming to grips that we as human beings are not only limited in our ability but also in our own capability. We must always depend upon Jesus for everything.

This is why it is vital to stay in the Word of God daily. We must never, ever misplace or allow ourselves to become disrobed from the full armor of God. We must stay alert. We must continue to ask the Lord to keep us in perfect peace, so we can be found with our minds on the Kingdom building of Jesus Christ. We must seek to know His will for our daily walk in this earth.

We must remember—just because Monday was spiritually successful, we cannot rest at ease and take our eyes off the real prize on Tuesday, thinking it will be the same. We must continue vigilance in our pursuit to maintain what our God died on the cross on our behalf to obtain through the blood of Jesus. We must learn how to contend for the victory we have through the Name of Jesus.

It is vital that we fully understand we do not have to fight for the victory. We already have it. We must stand still in Christ Jesus and protect that which God has already given to us, lest the enemy of this world quickly comes back and overtakes our minds and hearts with the worst news possible. He sometimes comes through social media outlets such as television, Instagram, Facebook and other outlets at the stroke of a button.

Haven't you ever wondered how you can be so happy first thing in the morning, walking around the house, singing your little praise and worship songs, perhaps hands are raised, quoting your scripture? And all within a matter of minutes, you stub your big toe, the cat scratches your good pantyhose, the car won't start or it starts, but you don't have enough gas to get where you're going. Now because of those minor incidentals, you are going to be late getting to your long-awaited scheduled impossible-to-get-in appointment that took four months to make in the first place. And now,

The Final Decision is Up to You

you've gone from being at ease to finding yourself stressed, frustrated, easily doused with a spirit of sadness, overwhelmed or carrying a sense of defeat. If you are not super careful, within moments you have travelled, spiritually speaking, from blessed and highly favored to "what just happened?"

What we think and meditate on for hours, especially if it is negative, can and most often will produce devastating effects on our health, mind, energy levels and general mood swings.

There were years in my life, sadly enough, I admit I cared entirely too much about what others thought of me, said about me, or even cared about me. At times, I allowed my mind to consider what the devil spoke into my ears rather than reading and resting in what God had already spoken over my life through His word.

Even when I knew the Word of God and what it said to me, where I made my biggest mistake was allowing the enemy to linger too long in my ear. Looking back now, I should have cast down those negative thoughts in the Name of Jesus the moment they began.

I should have never entertained for one second one lie from him, whether the thoughts were fact or not. God's Word is truth and it trumps every vicious lie and rumor the enemy brings to the table. What God says is the final Word over all.

> I now know for sure, that *"Finally, brothers, whatever is true, whatever is honorable, whatever is right, whatever is pure, whatever is lovely, whatever is*

admirable — if anything is excellent or praiseworthy — think on these things. Whatever you have learned and received and heard from me, and seen in me, put these things into practice. And the God of peace will be with you.

Philippians 4:8-9 (BSB)

This is absolutely true when I choose to think positively about another person. I am not guilt ridden or have to face them sheepishly. I don't have to hear in my heart what a fake I am, and how wrong I am afterward for pretending to like something or someone when all the while I know I don't.

As I grow closer to the Lord, I thank him every day to know it is not my place now, nor has it ever been, to go around condemning others whether things are fact or not. Gossip, lying, backbiting will never be acceptable to God It doesn't matter what I think about the person or how they act or respond to me. I am charged to love them—period.

I am definitely not advocating horrible behavior or rudeness from anyone. However, what I am saying now that I know how to exercise my choices. Either remove myself from the situation, walk away, or provide no response or input that will be misconstrued against me later. Best practices have demonstrated this in the past. Or I simply disassociate myself from the root cause altogether.

Today, it is so disheartening to know that countless individuals in the world literally thrive on gossip, dragging others names through the mud and speaking about things they have no real facts about. And even while they may have the proverbial rumor, praise our Almighty God, He is the only One with the true record. At the end of the day, His is the only one we have to give in account for.

Sometimes even when others have "their version of their truth," it still does not give them a right to speak it to anyone who would care to listen and to transport it to the masses. Those individuals have a problem with their hearts and find some sense of enjoyment from hurting, belittling and even attempting to damage the livelihoods, reputations and identities of others by any means necessary.

Some individuals never think twice about checking their heart condition before speaking, acting, lying, gossiping, or reacting. They make it their life's mission to go forth wreaking havoc as much as possible too as many people as they can. They never once consider the consequences of their actions, let alone take responsibility for their aftermath.

Let's look at the context of Ephesians 6:7-13.

> *With good will doing service, as to the Lord, and not to men: Knowing that whatsoever good thing any man doeth, the same shall he receive of the Lord, whether he be bond or free. And, ye masters, do the same things unto them, forbearing threatening: knowing that your Master also is in heaven; neither is there respect of persons with him. Finally, my brethren, be strong in the Lord, and in the power of his might. Put on the whole armour of God, that ye may be able to stand against the wiles of the devil. For we wrestle not against flesh and blood, but against principalities,*

> *against powers, against the rulers of the darkness of this world, against spiritual wickedness in high places. Wherefore take unto you the whole armour of God, that ye may be able to withstand in the evil day, and having done all, to stand. (KJV)*

I read a comment about a gentleman who stated after reading this particular passage of scripture "*...that this particular scripture reference was written to those who are in Christ and not to those who "profess" with their mouths to be a Christian but who does not reflect behaviors, mindset or lifestyles of a Christian ever.*

While I suppose that is one way of looking at it, it is still very frightening to be born again, yet choose to teeter between two dimensions in terms of confessing with our mouths to be saved but living as though there is no personal relationship, commitment or a greater responsibility to kingdom building at all.

Whether we know or understand it, once we are born again, we have an obligation of the services we render unto God and certainly to our fellow men. That service starts the moment we are born again. I believe we can only render unto God at our highest level when our minds and hearts are open to receive from God the wisdom, knowledge, direction and guidance only He can provide to us to share with others.

Chapter 22 - Becoming Kingdom Minded For Kingdom Purpose

I appeal to you therefore, brothers, by the mercies of God, to present your bodies as a living sacrifice, holy and acceptable to God, which is your spiritual worship. Do not be conformed to this world, but be transformed by the renewal of your mind, that by testing you may discern what is the will of God, what is good and acceptable and perfect.

Romans 12:1-2 (ESV)

Today, more than ever, the number one desire as Christians should be to reflect more of Christ and the strategic building plan of God's Kingdom for our individual lives. Focus on Him rather than concentrate our precious time on the everyday mundane pressures and stresses of this world that keep us bound to the personal affairs of what's trending in our world today.

I believe the heartbeat of what God desires for his children is coming into real maturity of what pleases God first and our being watchful to live a life and lifestyle that will cause the work of the Kingdom to move forward in a progressive and eternal manner. Our focus should be to please God with our walk while on earth.

And the only way to measure that is to become Kingdom-Minded concerning the things of God in realizing what's at stake here. In the book of Daniel 7:14, we find that the Kingdom of Heaven is the promise God gives to every believer. According to Daniel, He gave a glimpse of the future Kingdom to the Jews. In this book, The Son of Man was given dominion and a Kingdom that shall be everlasting.

So the most important thing that should be on the mind of a believer is the anticipation of the future Kingdom, establishing hope in the hearts of all believers no matter what problems befall us. And in today's times, there are many. For those of us who have hope for a New Kingdom, we will able to persevere even while living in tumultuous, wretched, ungodly, perilous times.

Some may ask how we can maintain hope in a Kingdom we have never seen when life as we know it still offers oppression, grief, heartache and even death daily. Are we just supposed to pretend life isn't happening before our very own eyes? Are we supposed to carry on with our day as if everything is okay?

Jesus said, "The kingdom of God does not come with observation; nor, will they say, 'See here!' or 'See there!' For indeed, the kingdom of God is within you." Luke 17:20-21 (NKJV)

If we want the same hope that does not wither with the pressures of time, if we want a steadfast confidence and total trust in a God that will never, ever leave, forsake or forget

The Final Decision is Up to You

about us, we need to understand the message of the Kingdom of God. The message of the Kingdom was one of the first messages our Lord and Savior Jesus Christ preached, and so did the apostles.

"Now after that John was put in prison, Jesus came into Galilee, preaching the gospel of the kingdom of God And saying, The time is fulfilled, and the kingdom of God is at hand: repent ye, and believe the gospel." Mark 1:14-15 (NKJV)

If the church (which is born-again believers of Jesus Christ), is to become Kingdom-Minded in order to be prepared for Kingdom building, we've got to become solid in our convictions of who we are and our purpose for being placed into the Kingdom of God in the first place.

The reason Jesus preached the gospel of the Kingdom was because it should be the desire of every believer first to serve Him in whatever capacity that is relevant to the Kingdom. The prayer we often call the Lord's Prayer states "thy kingdom come." We should look for and desire the Kingdom of God to manifest itself on earth through our daily living and serving.

So what is the Kingdom in the first place? The Kingdom is God's will being done on earth through mankind. The Kingdom is being subjected to a righteous leader. The Kingdom is joy and peace in the Holy Spirt (Romans 14:17). It is not based on man's reputation before other men, but it is based on a person's ability to submit to the will of God for their life.

Jesus Christ said the Kingdom of God is within you. (Luke 17:21) Behold what love the Heavenly Father has for us that He would deposit His Kingdom within us—healings, miracles and whatever else we need—He has already given it to us. To be Kingdom-minded is not only to think about God's presence here on earth, it is also to receive what He has for us to make it into His Kingdom.

In the Book of Luke 18:29-30, He said unto them, "Verily I say unto you, There is no man that hath left house, or parents, or brethren, or wife, or children, for the kingdom of God's sake, who shall not receive manifold (various, diverse and assorted), more in this present time, and in the world to come life everlasting." (KJV)

However, the one condition that goes with the Kingdom is repentance (a change of heart and mind toward something). Without repentance, we cannot enter into the Kingdom of God. It is the righteousness of God that propels (pushes, drives, forces, boosts and thrusts) us into His Kingdom

"But seek ye first the kingdom of God, and his righteousness; and all these things shall be added unto you." Matthew 6:33 (KJV)

Not only does repentance produce righteousness, but it also adds unto us the things we need. In other words, repentance provides for us the incentive to receive good things from God that should lead us into righteousness. God wants to give us the Kingdom (Luke 12:32) but we must be willing to receive the Kingdom by changing our lives through our mindset.

When we see the miracles and wonders of our time, we know the Kingdom of God is nigh (Matthew 12:28). The Jews were also witnesses to the miracles of God, but because they refused to repent, Matthew 21:43 states the Kingdom was taken from them "and given to a nation bringing forth the fruits thereof."

Let us not be misled by looking to the god of this world and having the Kingdom taken from us. Instead, let us look unto the one that is able to keep us from falling and present us faultless in the Kingdom of His dear Son. We must stop looking for answers in the world's system when God has already given us answers in Him.

When we do that, we can accomplish Philippians 2:5. *"Let this mind be in you, which was also in Christ Jesus."* (KJV)

1. Building the Kingdom of God at Home

"And do not be conformed to this world, but be transformed by the renewing of your mind, so that you may prove what the will of God is, that which is good and acceptable and perfect." Romans 12:2 (NASB)

2. Building the Kingdom of God in our Personal Lives
3. Building the Kingdom of God at Work
4. Building the Kingdom of God in our Community
5. We can build the Kingdom of God at large

Chapter 23 - Personal Take-a-Ways

How do you handle your personal anguish?

_____
_____
_____
_____
_____
_____
_____
_____

Is God considered the first person you turn to in times of trouble?

_____
_____
_____
_____
_____
_____
_____
_____

Is letting go of your past good, bad, difficult or too painful for you?

_____
_____
_____
_____
_____
_____
_____
_____

Why?

_____
_____
_____
_____
_____
_____
_____
_____

What real purpose does holding on to mental anguish, hatred, or malice serve you?

Do you have a tendency of holding on to what no longer feeds your soul spiritually?

Have you ever asked yourself what payoff or benefit you receive from past failures?

_____

_____

_____

_____

_____

_____

_____

Do you consider yourself trapped in your past with nowhere else to turn?

_____

_____

_____

_____

_____

_____

_____

Have you ever thought about the possibility of being free from it all?

_____
_____
_____
_____
_____
_____
_____
_____

Have you ever asked yourself what's stopping you from doing so?

_____
_____
_____
_____
_____
_____
_____
_____

The Final Decision is Up to You

Have you ever felt like giving up when things got worse before better?

___

Have you ever consider the possibility of being free from your past?

___

Do you the risk is too great too even try?

Do you think that true joy and happiness are a possibility?

The Final Decision is Up to You

Do you believe you are worthy of the blessings and hope God has for you?

_____
_____
_____
_____
_____
_____
_____
_____

Do you believe in hoping?

_____
_____
_____
_____
_____
_____
_____
_____

Why did my life turn out this way?

_____
_____
_____
_____
_____
_____
_____
_____

Do you believe the pain and suffering you may be enduring now is all your fault?

_____
_____
_____
_____
_____
_____
_____
_____

Are you content with waiting for the other person(s) to come to you to apologize first?

_____
_____
_____
_____
_____
_____
_____

Even when you haven't done anything wrong, do you spend your time believing, "Why should I still forgive first?"

_____
_____
_____
_____
_____
_____
_____

Have you ever said, "I'm okay. I don't need anybody else. I can make it own my own?"

_____
_____
_____
_____
_____
_____
_____
_____

Do you recognize the fact that you are suffering silently alone?

_____
_____
_____
_____
_____
_____
_____
_____

Are you ashamed or embarrassed to ask others for help or prayer?

_____
_____
_____
_____
_____
_____
_____

Have you ever wondered, "Where was God in all of my suffering and pain?"

_____
_____
_____
_____
_____
_____
_____

Do you believe God really cares about you?

_____
_____
_____
_____
_____
_____
_____

Do you really think He knows and fully understands your pain, hurt and disappointments?

_____
_____
_____
_____
_____
_____
_____

The Final Decision is Up to You

Have you asked yourself, "Why should I trust God with my sufferings?"

_____
_____
_____
_____
_____
_____
_____
_____

What do I do now after I have confessed to Him and/or to others?

_____
_____
_____
_____
_____
_____
_____
_____

Is forgiveness necessary?

What Was the Purpose of the Pain?

The Final Decision is Up to You

Are you struggling with unforgiveness & suffering?

_____
_____
_____
_____
_____
_____
_____
_____

Have you considered turning it over to God?

_____
_____
_____
_____
_____
_____
_____
_____

Looking ahead through a different perspective, what do you envision for your life?

___

Don't Cast Away Your Confidence in God

___

Trust God with your past as you move forward into your promising future.

There will be no more wasted energy.

Do you believe that all things are working for your good?

___

The sweet side of victory. What does that look like for you?

___

The Final Decision is Up to You

No More Delays…What do you plan to do about it?

_____
_____
_____
_____
_____
_____
_____
_____

What was the personal overview or take away for you in *Forgetting Former Things: The Power of Letting Go?*

_____
_____
_____
_____
_____
_____
_____
_____

Do you believe you can trust God in all things concerning your life?

_____
_____
_____
_____
_____
_____
_____

What does it mean to you to cast all of your care upon the Lord because He cares for you?

_____
_____
_____
_____
_____
_____
_____

Am I supposed to believe that after I cast all of my cares upon God, I am free to move forward without any burdens at all?

_____
_____
_____
_____
_____
_____
_____

What if I still feel the same in my emotions? Then what?

_____
_____
_____
_____
_____
_____
_____
_____

How will I know if I am fully healed from my past?

_____
_____
_____
_____
_____
_____
_____

How do I began to move forward in newness?

_____
_____
_____
_____
_____
_____
_____

How do I began to allow others into my heart and my life after I have been hurt and wounded?

Can I really trust God with my heart and my deepest desires?

What happens if the other person never accepts my apology? Am I still stuck?

_____
_____
_____
_____
_____
_____
_____
_____

What if they never apologize to me for the damage or the hurt they caused?

_____
_____
_____
_____
_____
_____
_____
_____

Is it really true that if I do not forgive them, God will not forgive me?

Isn't letting go of my past hurts and pains simply allowing myself vulnerability again for the next level of pain?

What is my guarantee that I will never be hurt again?

I really want to let it go, but honestly, I am too afraid to do it alone. What should I do?

Is letting go a process or must it be done right now?

_____
_____
_____
_____
_____
_____
_____

What are some of the ways I can expect to grow personally after letting go of the past?

_____
_____
_____
_____
_____
_____
_____
_____

What if the other person doesn't change?

The Final Decision is Up to You

This page intentionally left blank for any additional notes or thoughts the reader may want to record.

References

AlanP. (2011, May 1). *Developing God Confidence.* Retrieved from God is My Source!: http://www.godismysource.org/other-articles/developing-god-confidence

Alcorn, R. (2009). *If God is Good.* Danvers, MA, USA: Multnomah.

Chesterton, G. K. (1908). *Orthodoxy.* New York: John Lane Company.

Clark, C. S. (1946). *The Great Divorce.* New York: HarperCollins Publishers.

Clayton, J. N. (2007-2015). *Are There Really Benefits of Pain and Suffering.* Retrieved from Why Pain and Suffering?: http://www.whypain.org/benefits_of_pain.html

Curran, D. (2014, May 2). *Psalm 23: The Lord is My Shepherd.* Retrieved from PC:Purpose City: https://purposecity.com/insights/psalm-23-shepherd/

Elwell, W. A. (1996). *Baker's Evangelical Dictionary.* Grand Rapids: Baker Books a division of Baker Book House Company.

Experts, Y. (2017, July 17). *World of Psychology: Unpack Your Emotional Baggage to Help Your Body Heal.* Retrieved from Psyche Central: https://psychcentral.com/blog/unpack-your-emotional-baggage-to-help-your-body-heal/

Frankl, V. E. (1959, 1962, 1984, 1992, 2006). *Man's Search for Meaning.* Boston: Beacon Press.

Keller, T. (2013). *Walking with God Through Pain and Suffering.* New York: Penguin Group (USA) LLC.

Kreeft, P. (1986). *Making Sense Out of Suffering.* Ann Arbor: Servant Books.

Lewis, C. S. (1963). *A Grief Observed.* New York: Seabury Press.

Manning, B. (2004). *A Glimpse of Jesus.* New York, NY, USA: Harper Collins.

Ortlund, G. (n.d.). *A Deeper Look at What the Bible Says About Pain and Suffering.* Retrieved from Explore God: https://www.exploregod.com/what-the-bible-says-about-pain-and-suffering-paper

Randles, P. B. (2010, September 13). *Why Hope Maketh Not Ashamed...Romans 5.* Retrieved from Pastor Bill Randles Blog Post: https://billrandles.wordpress.com/2010/09/13/why-hope-maketh-not-ashamed-romans-5/

Rogers, A. (2010, July 6). *Do All Things Work Together for Good?* Retrieved from Billy Graham Evangelistic Association: https://billygraham.org/story/do-all-things-work-together-for-good/

Tada, J. E. (2000). *When God Weeps.* Grand Rapids: Zondervan.

Thinkmap, Inc. (n.d.). *Vocabulary.com Dictionary.* Retrieved from Vocabular.com: https://www.vocabulary.com/dictionary/anguish

Webster. (n.d.). *KJV Dictionary Definition.* Retrieved from The King James Bible Page: http://av1611.com/kjbp/kjv-dictionary/anguish.html

About the Author

Brenda is the Founder of Innovative Ministries, Inc., and the author and publisher of three books: *Had It Not Been For The Lord On Her Side*, *Raw Faith* and this latest release, *Forgetting Former Things, The Power of Letting Go*.

Brenda writes about the struggles and unnecessary weight and perils of carrying around generational baggage, unforgiveness, hidden pain and worldly stressors that over time can cause significant damage to our emotional, physical and spiritual wellbeing in addition to our peace and joy being hindered in our daily walk with God.

Known for her spiritual wit, depth, and down-to-earth style, Brenda weaves colorful illustrations and humor along with biblical truth to help audiences find contentment, assuredness and endurance with the Lord. Through Brenda's signature wit and poignant story-telling, audiences are prompted to look beyond their circumstances and life situations to embrace, explore and receive the experiences of God's wonderful grace and mercy in the midst of adversity.

In her personal life and through her intimate walk with Christ, Brenda is discovering that every new day is a glorious fresh gift from God our heavenly Father to start afresh and anew! Brenda truly believes that as sons and daughters of the Most High God, we can be confident, courageous and self-reliant in the fact that Jesus Christ, our Lord loves us beyond our human comprehension and to prove it; we only need to read the Word of God for ourselves and believe in Him alone to find out just how much He really cares about everything that concerns us.

www.ingramcontent.com/pod-product-compliance
Lightning Source LLC
Chambersburg PA
CBHW071945110426
42744CB00030B/290